An A-Z of Discipleship

An A-Z of Discipleship

Amy Parkin

The Christadelphian
404 Shaftmoor Lane, Hall Green, Birmingham B28 8SZ, UK

2021

First published 2018
Reprinted 2019, 2021

© 2021 The Christadelphian Magazine and Publishing Association

ISBN 978 0 85189 410 2 (print edition)
ISBN 978 0 85189 411 9 (electronic edition)

Printed and bound in the UK by
CMP (UK) Limited

All scripture quotations are from the English Standard Version (ESV) of the Bible, unless otherwise stated.

Scripture quotations marked (ESV) are from The Holy Bible, English Standard Version, copyright 2001 by Crossway Bibles, a division of Good News Publishers. Used by permission. All rights reserved.

Extracts from the Authorised Version of the Bible (The King James Bible), the rights in which are vested in the Crown, are reproduced by permission of the Crown's Patentee, Cambridge University Press.

Scripture quotations marked (CEV) are from the Contemporary English Version © 1991, 1992, 1995 by American Bible Society. Used by permission.

Scripture quotations and / or notes marked (NET©) are from the NET Bible® copyright ©1996-2016 by Biblical Studies Press, L.L.C. All rights reserved.

Scripture quotations marked (NIV) are from the Holy Bible, New International Version Anglicised. Copyright © 1979, 1984, 2011 Biblica. Used by permission of Hodder & Stoughton Ltd., an Hachette UK company. All rights reserved. 'NIV' is a registered trademark of Biblica. UK trademark number 1448790.

Scripture quotations marked (NKJV) are from the New King James Version®. Copyright © 1982 by Thomas Nelson Inc. Used by permission. All rights reserved.

Scripture quotations marked (TLB) are from The Living Bible, copyright © 1971. Used by permission of Tyndale House Publishers, Inc., Carol Stream, Illinois 60188. All rights reserved.

Contents

Preface vii

1. 'A' for Acceptance 1
2. 'B' for Balance 5
3. 'C' for Children of Light 11
4. 'D' for Decisions 17
5. 'E' for Exalt 25
6. 'F' for Fellowship 32
7. 'G' for Goal 40
8. 'H' for Humility 47
9. 'I' for Integrity 54
10. 'J' for Joy 61
11. 'K' for Know the Lord 69
12. 'L' for Loyalty 76

13. 'M' for Meditation 84

14. 'N' for Now 92

15. 'O' for Optimism 100

16. 'P' for Prayer 107

17. 'Q' for Quietness 114

18. 'R' for Reliance 123

19. 'S' for Sacrifice 131

20. 'T' for Thankfulness 138

21. 'U' for Unique 145

22. 'V' for Vision 152

23. 'W' for Words 159

24. 'X' for X-ray 167

25. 'Y' for Yoke 175

26. 'Z' for Zeal 182

Scripture index 191

Preface

THIS book began as a series of articles which ran in *The Christadelphian* from July 2015 to August 2017. Drawing from scripture and personal experience, each chapter addresses a different aspect of our walk as disciples of Christ. Though by no means exhaustive, it is hoped that readers of all ages and from all walks of life will find the subject matter both helpful and thought-provoking.

Practical books such as this one must, by nature, provide advice, guidance and suggestions. Though I have endeavoured to take a scripture-focused approach to every topic, there will always be a personal bias or perspective with which some readers may disagree. For this, I can make no apology, for without drawing from personal experience and from the experiences of friends and family, I would have little to add that could not be read directly from the pages of scripture.

I make no grand claims when it comes to my own walk, nor do I claim to be an expert on any of the twenty-six subjects covered in this book. We all, every day, fall short of the glory of God – yet Christ shows us a better way.

Discipleship is a journey – not a destination – and we make this journey together. We mature as disciples when we encounter trials and persevere; when we acknowledge our sin and work hard to turn things around; when we hit rock bottom and humbly ask God to lift us up; when we suffer great loss – and win Christ.

Amy Parkin
October 2018

Chapter 1
A for Acceptance

THERE is a well known prayer, known as the Serenity Prayer, which says:

"God, grant me the serenity to accept the things I cannot change, the courage to change the things I can, and the wisdom to know the difference."

It teaches that there are many things in life which we must graciously accept as our lot. Like it or not, we all have to work hard to put food on the table and keep a roof over our heads; we all have difficult decisions to make in life; we shall all, at some point, have to deal with illness and grief; we cannot avoid stress, hurt, disappointments, frustrations and setbacks. Life is rarely easy.

But surely that's the point. The day we were baptized, God could have said, 'Now that you're part of my family I'll make sure your life is as easy and as happy as possible. I'll give you a well-paid job (with no stress, no responsibilities and a two-hour lunch break), an amazing house (complete with housekeeper and personal chef), all the money you need, a devoted spouse, obedient children and twenty weeks' holiday a year. I'll make sure you never get ill and no one you love ever dies. I'll protect you from anything that might make you feel sad or uncomfortable and I'll make all your decisions for you so that you don't have to get stressed about them'. How thankful we are that He didn't! For, as appealing as such a life may sometimes seem, especially in the face of trials and suffering, we would soon become incredibly bored and complacent. We would have no real motivation to do anything, since we would take it for granted that everything was given to us on a plate. Not only this, but we would lose our free will, since God would be making our decisions for us. It would be easy to attribute our success to ourselves; our faith would stagnate and, with no challenges in life to cope with, we would lose out on countless opportunities for growth. We would never see or comprehend the need to "trust in the LORD with all [our] heart, and do not lean on [our] own understanding" (Proverbs 3:5). Thankfully, God knows that to give us everything we want would be to stunt our growth. It could turn us away from Him and spoil us irreparably.

The writer to the Hebrews instead exhorts us to embrace and accept the discipline of the Lord (Hebrews 12:5) – the hard times that come to test our faith – because this is an integral part of being a son or daughter of God. Verse 10 says that "he disciplines us for our good, *that we may share his holiness*", and goes on to explain that, though our trials and difficulties are unpleasant and painful now, and we can so often feel like giving up, the end result is righteousness (verse 11). These passages are telling us that we become more like our Heavenly Father and the Lord Jesus Christ when we patiently endure suffering. Conversely, without suffering it would be impossible to become more like them. We would remain just as naïvely self-centred and ungrateful as we were when we were children!

Good things

James adds that "the testing of [our] faith produces steadfastness ... that [we] may be perfect and complete, *lacking in nothing*" (James 1:3,4). God promises that, while He won't give us everything we want, He will give us everything we need. The Psalmist confirmed this when he wrote, "No good thing does he withhold from those who walk uprightly" (Psalm 84:11). Note that he says "no good thing". Only God knows what is truly good for us and will benefit us in the long run. We might feel that we are being denied certain things that we deem "good" – money, a family, the perfect job – but God has better things in mind. While it is true that He will make sure we have clothes on our backs and food for our mouths (Matthew 6:25-32), most of all He wants to give us love, joy, peace, patience, kindness, goodness, faithfulness, gentleness and self-control. These are things we have to learn and only He knows how best to teach us those things. It takes great faith to accept that God will supply all our needs, but there is remarkable peace and freedom that comes from knowing and believing this truth.

James goes on to say:

> "Blessed is the man who remains steadfast under trial, for when he has stood the test he will receive the crown of life, which God has promised to those who love him." (James 1:12)

Here, James implies that remaining faithful and resolute in the face of trials is one of the ways in which we can show God that we love Him. By accepting what is going on in our lives and perceiving it as a character-refining, faith-defining situation, where God is in control, and trusting Him completely, we show great love for our Father and He rewards us by giving us the crown of life. What greater reward could there be than eternal life, and what greater antidote to our present suffering could there be than this amazing hope?

In Romans we learn that "suffering produces endurance, and endurance produces character, and character produces hope, and hope does not put us to shame" (Romans 5:3-5). We can rejoice in our suffering, accepting that this is how God helps us to grow, embracing the perspective it gives us on life and how our present difficulties make us long more intensely for the kingdom. "For I consider", wrote Paul, "that the sufferings of this present time are not worth comparing with the glory that is to be revealed to us" (Romans 8:18).

Everything happens for a reason and we must believe and accept that God knows best, that He has a plan for our lives, and that through patient endurance we shall enter His kingdom. God knows our needs and our struggles and is working in our lives to help us learn from them and cope with them. Life is rarely easy, but by accepting that God is in control we can experience that wonderful "peace of God, which surpasses all understanding" (Philippians 4:7).

Questions and suggestions

- Can you think of a time during which your faith was tested and, as a result, you experienced personal and spiritual growth? How might the luxury of hindsight shape the way in which you view present trials?
- Is there a current problem in your life which you are struggling to accept? Spend time bringing your problem before God, who makes all things work together for the good of them that love Him.
- Take some time to meditate on the reward God has promised to those who remain steadfast under trial: eternal life. A clear goal provides powerful motivation and encouragement.

Chapter 2
B for Balance

WE often hear about the importance of maintaining a healthy work-life balance and there are hundreds of self-help books on the market addressing this issue from many different angles. As disciples of the Lord Jesus, it can often seem frustratingly difficult to maintain a healthy balance between the 'spiritual' and 'material' – but is such a balance possible, or even desirable?

Each one of us has responsibilities and commitments, be they at work, at home or within the ecclesia. We are businessmen, businesswomen, students, teachers, parents, grandparents, carers, homeowners, recording brothers, librarians, treasurers – all of us have a dozen roles to fill and few of us feel we really have the balance right between work commitments, responsibilities at home and our spiritual life. The world expects us to be successful students, ambitious employees, perfect housewives and social butterflies, and all the while we struggle with the added pressure of striving to be godly disciples of Christ. It might be tempting to see this added pressure as a burden and to envy those who only have a work-life balance to contend with but, as we shall see, God tells us that the 'spiritual' things in life should define us, rather than be a separate part of our already greatly divided lives.

Can God be compartmentalised?

When it comes to our relationship with God, we can so often use "being busy" as an excuse to skip the readings, miss the evening meeting or neglect to pray. We often bemoan our busy lives: "If only work wasn't so full-on, I'd be able to find a better balance between work and the meeting", or "The children are always up so early and then by the time they've gone to bed, I'm too tired to do the readings. Once they're a bit older, I'll find it much easier to strike a balance".

But what kind of a balance do we envisage? Do we seek to divide our time equally between God (i.e., reading, praying, serving), work and personal life? Do we go for a 50:25:25 approach, giving a reluctant nod towards the idea that God should be the priority in our life? Do we focus solely on work from nine to five, social and family life in the evenings and Saturdays, and God on Sundays?

In a world where many people desire to draw a clear line between work and home life, the idea of compartmentalising our lives in this way might seem like a sensible and practical solution, but we know deep down that God can't be compartmentalised and that any effort to divide up our time between the spiritual and the material is futile.

God never sleeps

The Bible's message is clear: we can't take a break from being sons and daughters of the living God, who Himself is always present and does not slumber or sleep (Jeremiah 23:24, Psalm 121:4). The Psalmist wrote:

> "Where shall I go from your Spirit? Or where shall I flee from your presence? If I ascend to heaven, you are there! If I make my bed in Sheol, you are there!" (Psalm 139:7,8)

So should we be seeking a balance at all? If God is everywhere and we are full-time disciples, surely our whole life should be God-focused. The balance should be tipped *entirely* in God's direction.

Christ in us

Rather than juggling the spiritual, personal and work-related elements of our lives, which often leaves us feeling both physically and spiritually exhausted, we are called to view every aspect of our lives as being part of a spiritual whole. We do this by making God and His standards an integral part of everything we do. After all, we are not living for ourselves, but for Christ and therefore for the Lord God:

> "For the love of Christ controls us, because we have concluded this: that one has died for all, therefore all have died; and he died for all, that those who live *might no longer live for themselves* but for him who for their sake died and was raised." (2 Corinthians 5:14,15)

Paul follows this idea further in Galatians, explaining that, "It is no longer I who live, but *Christ who lives in me*" (2:20). Everything we do, we do "for the Lord" (Colossians 3:23) as "ambassadors for Christ" (2 Corinthians 5:20), "to the glory of God" (1 Corinthians 10:31). This means that, whether we are taking the children to school, putting the bins out, giving a presentation at work, answering the phone or a million other things, we are doing these as Christ's representatives. The focus is *always* on the spiritual.

The Bible paints a clear picture of how a love of and obedience to God's word, along with fellowship, praise, prayer, thankfulness and service – all the things that Christ so perfectly demonstrated in his life – are to fill our lives too, since Christ is *in us* and our lives are no longer our own. If we are baptized, we "belong to Christ" (Mark 9:41). Our lives are not our own and we should not treat them as such. *How could we possibly devote only part of our lives to God, when our whole lives are His, through the Lord Jesus?*

"We have the mind of Christ"

The implications of this are all-encompassing. No longer do we need to regard life as a battle of priorities, a struggle to get the balance right. Instead, we can embrace the knowledge that everything we do and say is to be done "in the name of the Lord Jesus, giving thanks to God the Father through him" (Colossians 3:17). Our attitude should always reflect that of our Lord Jesus, since "we have the mind of Christ" (1 Corinthians 2:16). This means that we must always:

> "... walk in a manner worthy of the calling to which [we] have been called, with all humility and gentleness, with patience, bearing with one another in love, eager to maintain the unity of the Spirit in the bond of peace."
>
> (Ephesians 4:1-3)

Whether we are at work, at home or with our brothers and sisters, we should aim always to be aware of God's presence and strive to do our best and to be like the Lord Jesus. We must take every opportunity to talk about our faith and about God's word with our family, friends and colleagues. Our precious idle moments (time spent commuting, showering, waiting in queues, etc.) need not be idle, but can be spent in prayer or meditation. When problems arise at work, we can use scriptural principles to help solve them, and when our family is driving us up the wall, we can deal with them gently, as true imitators of Christ. Every moment of every day should be treated as a chance for growth and an opportunity to give glory to our Heavenly Father. In moments of anger, impatience or stress we can call to mind the words of the Apostle Paul, who exhorted the Galatians, saying, "Let us not grow weary of doing good" (Galatians 6:9) and told the Colossians that they should, "let the peace of Christ rule in [their] hearts ... And be thankful" (Colossians 3:15).

A difficult task

Living life in a constant state of awareness of God's presence, of our role as ambassadors for Christ, and of the knowledge that our lives are "hidden with Christ in God" (Colossians 3:3) is not something that comes naturally to us. We have to work at it every day and we shall often fail to maintain such a one-sided balance. The development of this kind of mindset takes a lifetime, so what better time to start than now?

Put it into practice

Here are a few practical suggestions to help you get started. You could try out one of these suggestions each week for the next few weeks and see what works for you. Once the first step has been made, the gathering momentum will make it easier to effect lasting changes.

- Make time each day for prayer.
- Choose a passage of scripture to meditate upon and pray about.
- Memorise scripture.
- Do one portion of the daily readings each mealtime.
- If you eat on your own, pray for the duration of your mealtimes.
- Pray every time you're in a queue.

- Pray each morning about your upcoming day, asking God for His support, guidance and protection, and acknowledging that only He knows how your day will turn out.
- Tell God everything you are thankful for (even the tiny things) and all that you hope for (especially the big things).
- Stick your favourite Bible verses up around the house.
- Pay attention to the world around you and marvel at its beauty.
- Get excited about the signs of the times: do some research!
- Talk to your brothers and sisters about the kingdom.
- See your spiritual responsibilities as things you are happy to do because they give God so much glory.
- Call an elderly brother or sister; better still, visit them.
- Talk to your colleagues about a recent Bible talk you've heard.
- Find time to take a step back from your life and focus on the "one thing" that really matters (see Philippians 3:13; Psalm 27:4).

Questions and suggestions

- Do you compartmentalise your life?
- Are there times you tell yourself you're "too busy" to do the readings or attend an ecclesial meeting or event? Is that really true? If it is, what changes could you make so that you have time for the things that really matter?
- Choose an area of your life that you wouldn't normally consider in a spiritual context and commit it to God in prayer. Purpose to give Him glory in every aspect of your life.

Chapter 3
C for Children of Light

JESUS declared, "I am the light of the world" (John 8:12) and he also said that his disciples are the light of the world (Matthew 5:14), but what does it mean to walk in the light, to be "children of light" (1 Thessalonians 5:5)?

We find light in both the very first and the very last chapters of the Bible. When God said, "Let there be light" (Genesis 1:3) He wasn't referring to the sun, which was created on the fourth day. The light created on the first day was called "Day" and its counterpart, darkness, was called "Night" and these themes can be found in 1 Thessalonians 5:5 where we read, "For you are all children of light, children of the day. We are not of the night or of the darkness". In Revelation 22, we read that the "night will be no more. They will need no light of lamp or sun, for the Lord God will be their light ..." (verse 5). In the previous chapter, we learn that New Jerusalem will have "no need of sun or moon to shine on it, for the glory of God gives it light, and its lamp is the Lamb" (21:23). From this we can infer that the light is the light of God's glory and that Jesus (the Lamb), in perfectly manifesting God's character and purpose, became a lamp which shone His radiant light into the world. As children of light – children of God – we should always be seeking to manifest His character and truth, shining as lights in a world of darkness that does not know Him, a city on a hill, a beacon of blazing light that cannot be hidden.

Not only does light represent God's glory, but throughout the Bible it is often paralleled with life. Job asked, "Why is light given to him who is in misery, and life to the bitter in soul?" (Job 3:20). Speaking about the day of his birth, Job declared, "Let that day be darkness! May God above not seek it, nor light shine upon it" (verse 4). He was surely alluding to the fact that in the womb there is utter darkness, but when we are born we are brought into the light. We see by extension that darkness is connected with death and the grave, and light with life. There is a parallel here with our own lives: before our baptism (our rebirth) we were living in darkness and our only destination was the grave, but now we live in God's light and we have the hope of everlasting life.

Walk in the light

Peter picked up on this when he wrote that God has "called [us] out of darkness into his marvellous light" (1 Peter 2:9), and Paul too, in his letter to the Ephesians wrote, "for at one time you were in darkness, but now you are light in the Lord. Walk as children of light" (Ephesians 5:8). This idea of walking in the light first appears in Psalm 56:13 where the Psalmist writes, "For you have delivered my soul from death … that I may walk before God in the light of life". Walking in the light is different from simply sitting in the light and basking in its warmth. It is an active, rather than a passive, state and we have to make a conscious decision to get up and walk. If we walk in the light of life, we allow God's light to guide our steps and give our lives direction and meaning. The idea of this light guiding us along the true path is illustrated in Psalm 119:105 where we read,

"Your word is a lamp to my feet and a light to my path". We think too about how Jesus described himself not just as the "light of the world", but also as "the way, and the truth, and the life" (John 14:6). He manifested God's light – His glorious character and purpose – so that we would know which path (or "way") our lives should take, leading to eternal life.

Psalm 119:105 is of further interest to us because it parallels God's word with light. The scriptures are a very real and powerful manifestation of God's will and purpose with the earth, of His character and glory, and of His light. As we read the Bible we gain wisdom and understanding, which light our path. The Apostle Paul called it the "word of life" (Philippians 2:16) because this light brings everlasting life. Writing to the Corinthians, he wrote of "the light of the gospel of the glory of Christ, who is the image of God" (2 Corinthians 4:4). This further demonstrates to us that the glory of God, which the Lord Jesus perfectly manifested to the world, is a light. The Gospel, or 'good news', shines forth as a beacon from the Lord Jesus Christ and it should shine from us too, if we really are children of light.

Put on the armour of light

So how do we become children of light? First of all, we must believe in Jesus, who himself said:

> "I have come into the world as light, so that whoever believes in me may not remain in darkness [...] While you have the light, believe in the light, that you may become 'sons of light.'" (John 12:46,36)

Once we have this belief, we need actively to "cast off the works of darkness and put on the armour of light" (Romans 13:12). This is something we can only do if we learn to differentiate between darkness and light. Since Jesus completely manifested God's light in everything he said and did, we can look to the Bible record of his life and try faithfully to follow his example, as well as the examples of the countless faithful men and women in the scriptures who loved God's law and strove to walk in the light. By doing this, we too will find strength to walk in the light of life, not turning aside onto darkened pathways that lead to sin and death.

We are not of darkness

Those of us who have been baptized have undertaken to strive for the rest of our lives to be children of light and not of darkness. This is not something to be taken lightly. When Jesus returns to judge us, "as servants of Christ and stewards of the mysteries of God", he will "bring to light the things now hidden in darkness and will disclose the purposes of the heart" (1 Corinthians 4:1,5). We need to take care, then, to examine our lives and to remove any darkness. Though we may be able to convince those around us, and often even ourselves, that we are full of good works and that there are no hidden sins, God sees through the façade. Nothing we do is in secret. Even when we think we are alone, with the curtains drawn and the door shut, God sees. Even if we don't say aloud the things we are thinking, God knows.

> "If I say, 'Surely the darkness shall cover me, and the light about me be night,' even the darkness is not dark to you; the night is bright as the day, for the darkness is as light with you." (Psalm 139:11,12)

David knew from experience that nothing can be hidden from God.

In Ephesians, we are exhorted:

> "Take no part in the unfruitful works of darkness, but instead expose them. For it is shameful even to speak of the things that they do in secret. But when anything is exposed by the light, it becomes visible, for anything that becomes

visible is light. Therefore it says, 'Awake, O sleeper, and arise from the dead, and Christ will shine on you.'" (5:11-14)

What are these "unfruitful works of darkness"? Who are the ones doing things in secret? Could this refer to you – or me? It can be tempting to skip over the more unsavoury passages of scripture – the verses that talk about the things we shouldn't be doing. We love to read in Galatians 5:22,23 of the fruit of the Spirit, but do we pay as much attention to the preceding verses about the works of the flesh? If we want to walk as children of light, we have to take care to expose the unfruitful works of darkness in our own lives.

"Now the works of the flesh are evident: sexual immorality, impurity, sensuality, idolatry, sorcery, enmity, strife, jealousy, fits of anger, rivalries, dissensions, divisions, envy, drunkenness, orgies, and things like these."
(Galatians 5:19-21)

At the breaking of bread, and indeed throughout the week, we need to examine ourselves and ask, Are any of these things taking over my life? Do I think about any of these things, or enjoy watching other people commit these sins? If the answer is 'yes', we need to work hard to cut these things out of our lives and fill the space instead with the fruit of the Spirit: love, joy, peace, patience, kindness, goodness, faithfulness, gentleness and self-control. Our prayer should be:

"Search me, O God, and know my heart! Try me and know my thoughts! And see if there be any grievous way in me, and lead me in the way everlasting!" (Psalm 139:23,24)

A city on a hill

We are a city on a hill, shining God's light into a world of darkness. As children of light and of the day, we have a responsibility to rid our lives of any darkness so that we can shine brightly as witnesses to those around us of God's glorious character and purpose with the earth. God's word is a light to our path, guiding us to the kingdom. Soon, this dark night will be over and we shall watch as the sun rises, heralding the start of a new and everlasting day when the true light of God's glory will shine forth from Jerusalem, the literal "city on a hill", and fill the whole earth.

Questions and suggestions

- Are you ready to walk in the light? How will you shine God's light to those around you this week?
- Could any of the works of the flesh in Galatians 5:19-21 be applied to your life? Take time to lay these struggles before God, and seek encouragement from His word.
- Meditate on the opening verses of Ephesians 5 and lift your thinking above the works of the flesh. Determine to be a child of light, not of darkness.

Chapter 4
D for Decisions

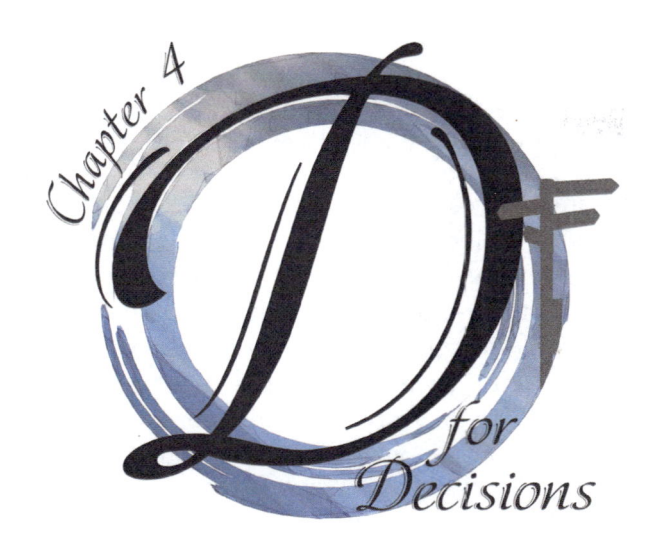

IN life, the decisions we make generally fall into two categories: black and white decisions where right and wrong choices are clearly defined, and those often pivotal decisions where all choices seem equally valid. In this article we address both of these and consider ways in which we, as disciples of Christ, might tackle them.

Black and white

More than any generation that has gone before us, we are daily bombarded with messages from the TV and media that entice us to enjoy all the temptations the world has to offer – to do what feels good, what we deem to be right, and to choose whatever will bring us the most happiness and success.

Thankfully, we have a much more detailed guide to right and wrong. The Bible clearly defines God's standards, from the ten commandments to the fruit of the Spirit; from the wise words of Proverbs to the letters to the seven ecclesias in Revelation.

The question we must ask ourselves is: do I spend more time reading and thinking about God's standards, or the world's?

Each time we read the scriptures, we feed our minds with sound advice and internalise more of what God says about right and wrong. As a result, our consciences are strengthened against what the world says so that we are increasingly able to stand up for what we know to be right. On the other side, if we spend more time watching and reading about the world's standards than we do absorbing God's word, we should not be surprised if the lines between black and white begin to blur.

To take two extreme examples, the world tells us that promiscuity is acceptable – 'just do what is best for you, what makes you happy' – but the Bible tells us the complete opposite:

> "The body is not meant for sexual immorality, but for the Lord, and the Lord for the body." (1 Corinthians 6:13)

Drunkenness may not be seen as a problem, but Proverbs tell us:

> "Wine is a mocker, strong drink a brawler, and whoever is led astray by it is not wise." (20:1)

In Galatians we read that the works of the flesh include both sexual immorality and drunkenness and that "those who do such things will not inherit the kingdom of God" (5:19,21). It can be so difficult to do the right thing when those around us are choosing otherwise. But far worse than blindly doing the wrong thing would be *knowingly* to do that.

Dealing with temptation

And this is where things get difficult. Sometimes, choosing to do the right thing is easy. Our friend eats our last Rolo when we're not looking and we choose to laugh about it rather than fly into a fit of rage. Someone cuts in front of us at the checkout and we wisely choose not to wrestle them to the ground. But what if we *want* to do the wrong thing? What if it's appealing to the flesh and we're finding it hard to resist?

When Jesus spent forty days and nights in the wilderness, he experienced extreme amounts of temptation. Although only three specific moments of temptation are recorded for us in the Gospels, these were almost certainly not isolated events, but rather give us an insight into the constant battle that waged as the spirit was determined to obey God but the flesh desperately wanted to satisfy its own desires. Each time, the Lord Jesus combats temptation with scripture, taking the advice of the Psalmist who wrote, "I have stored up your word in my heart, that I might not sin against you" (Psalm 119:11). The advice here is clear: we must diligently read God's word and allow it to take root in our hearts.

I recently discovered some old proof books at our meeting room and was encouraged to start memorising 'proofs' again. It is surprising how little time it takes to memorise just a few verses, and yet the impact is huge: these verses are now readily available when I need to call them to mind. My challenge to readers for the coming month is to memorise one short passage a week and observe the difference it makes in your life – the subtle shift in perspective and the extra layer of armour in the fight against temptation.

The power of prayer

In the Garden of Gethsemane, during his last hours of mental and physical agony, the Lord Jesus lovingly gave his disciples a final piece of advice: "Watch and pray that you may not enter into temptation" (Matthew 26:41). That night, Jesus knelt and *prayed* for God's will to be done, not his own. We too need to cast our burden on the Lord, believing that He will sustain us (Psalm 55:22). Jesus understood the power of prayer and we should never underestimate just how powerfully God can work in our lives too, if only we would ask. "Whatever you ask in prayer", Jesus said, "you will receive, if you have faith" (Matthew 21:22).

Even with a wealth of sound scriptural advice as to how we should live our lives, when faced with a choice between right and wrong, the easiest choice to make is often the wrong one. It takes great faith, courage and integrity to make the right decision, but we can be confident that there is rejoicing in heaven when we choose actively to shun temptation and pursue righteousness. No prayer for strength in the face of temptation will ever go unheard.

Fear of making the 'wrong' decision

So far we have considered decisions that involve easily discernible (to the Bible reader, at least) right and wrong choices. What then of decisions where all choices appear to be equally valid, equally 'right' and none would cause us or those around us to sin? Whilst these decisions don't cause us the agony of temptation, they do often paralyse us into a state of indecision or procrastination. We may be so afraid of making the 'wrong' decision that we fail to make any decision at all. Even after making a decision, we can end up consumed with guilt or regret, or with nostalgia for what could have been.

One problem here is that we assume there was a right decision in the first place. If two choices of action are equally valid, then sometimes we simply have to make a decision and be happy with it. We should of course do this prayerfully and with a sensible degree of care, but ultimately we need to stop procrastinating and make the decision.

God knows the decisions we shall make and they already form part of His plan for us. Whether we feel, in our flawed and short-sighted opinion, that they were good decisions or bad ones, if we are humble and prepared to learn from our mistakes, all decisions can help us to grow.

Identity crisis

In addition to the fear that we shall make the 'wrong' decision, there is also the fear that the big decisions we make will change who we are: if we decide one thing, we become one person, and if we decide another, we become a different person. This is particularly acute when it comes to deciding between things like university courses and career paths, but also when choosing where to move, which ecclesia to join, who to marry and so many other important decisions. In many cases, there may not be a clearly defined right or wrong answer, but the decision we do make will impact upon many facets of our lives.

In the face of all of this, we can find reassurance that our decisions do not define who we are: God does. We have been created in His image (Genesis 1:27), we are His temple (1 Corinthians 6:19) and our lives are "hidden with Christ in God" (Colossians 3:3). We are "a chosen people, a royal priesthood, a holy nation, a people belonging to God" (1 Peter 2:9, NIV). We are "children of God" (1 John 3:2). This is who we are and who we always will be, as long as we remain faithful. Our identity in Christ should define our decisions. So how can we put this into practice?

Acknowledge Him

When making any decision, and that includes situations where there is no real right or wrong choice, the word of God offers an abundance of sound advice. In Proverbs 3:5,6 we are counselled:

"Trust in the LORD with all your heart, and do not lean on your own understanding. In all your ways acknowledge him, and he will make straight your paths."

When faced with any kind of decision, we should first of all take it to God in prayer, acknowledging that we cannot make the decision on our own because only He knows the end from the beginning. Sometimes, prayerful consideration of a decision is enough and we are able confidently to choose between one path and another. Other times, we still won't feel a pull in any particular direction. This is when we truly have to acknowledge God in all our ways. This is the time to sit down and really weigh up the pros and cons. Some things to consider for each possible path would be:

- Will this decision bring me closer to God or push me further away?
- Will I have enough time for God (prayer, reading, for example)?
- Does past experience (or the experience of others) suggest one option may be better than the others?
- Will I be able to get to the Sunday meeting and Bible Class or will I be too busy / tired / live too far away?
- Is there anything that might cause me to have to compromise on matters of conscience?
- What kind of people will I be spending my time with? (Consider the advice of Psalm 1.)
- Are my motives godly or worldly (i.e., am I seeking to grow and to help others to grow, or am I seeking success / recognition)?
- Is there a better option, with a bigger impact for my discipleship?

With all of this information, hopefully the best option will become clear, but sometimes there might still seem to be no obvious answer. If a decision has to be made within a certain time frame, then sometimes all there is left to do is to pray, choose, pray some more and trust that God will guide the outcome.

On the other hand, if the decision does not need to be made immediately, or even really at all, then we should consider that God's answer may be 'No' or 'Not yet'. We might *want* to move to a new area, change jobs or change ecclesia, but if the decision is proving too difficult to make, perhaps it is a decision for another time and we should instead work hard to make the most of our current situation, learning to be content with the things with which God has so richly blessed us.

Seek first the kingdom

Above all, we must strive with every decision to love the Lord our God with all our heart, soul, mind and strength (Mark 12:30), and to "seek first the kingdom of God and his righteousness" (Matthew 6:33). Whilst we should not purposefully make bad decisions, if we can truly say that we have put God first, we need not worry disproportionately about the potential consequences of a decision (financial hardship, losing friends, receiving unjust blame or disapproval).

If we focus on the righteousness of God and seek to be like Him, living today as if we were already in the kingdom and fixing our eyes on that future hope, then God will grant us all that we need.

Questions and suggestions

- Can you think of a time when you used society's compromising standards of "do what feels right" and

"look out for number one" to make a decision? What was the result? What did you learn from that experience?
- Are there times when you want to do the wrong thing? Times when temptation is strong? Find relevant and helpful passages of scripture to memorise, and prepare your mind and heart for battle.
- Is there a decision you are putting off because you are afraid of making the wrong decision? Now is the time to take action!

Chapter 5
E for Exalt

THERE are several Hebrew words that are translated "exalt" or "exalted" in our English Bibles. Collectively, they mean to lift up, hold up, raise, set on high, promote, esteem highly and to prize. They can also refer to loftiness, haughtiness, arrogance and pride. Interestingly, the Hebrew word most often translated "exalt[ed]" (*ruwm*) in the King James Version is even more frequently translated "lift[ed] up" (sixty-three times), so exalting someone or something is all about lifting them higher and putting them in the most prominent position in our lives, giving them all praise, glory and honour.

Putting God first

As you might expect, the book which refers the most to the act of exalting God is the book of Psalms. Here, the Psalmist proclaims with joy and passion:

> "Be *exalted*, O LORD, in your strength! We will sing and praise your power." (21:13)

> "The LORD is *high above* all nations, and his glory above the heavens!" (113:4)

> "Be *exalted*, O God, above the heavens! Let your glory be over all the earth!" (57:5)

The Psalmist places a particular emphasis on exalting God's name and His word (both of which reveal His purpose to us):

> "For you have exalted above all things *your name and your word.*" (138:2)

> "Let them praise *the name of the LORD*, for *his name* alone is exalted; his majesty is above earth and heaven." (148:13)

As Bible students, we know that God's name is closely bound up with His plan and purpose. His word is the record we have of this plan, and we know that everything God speaks is true and right. Exalting His name and His word involves putting God's plan first: trusting that He knows the end from the beginning; accepting that our own plans are flawed and short-sighted, but that His purpose is eternal.

If we are truly to exalt God "above the heavens", if God truly takes the highest place in our lives, there can be no room for other people or activities to take priority. We must constantly be aware of His exalted position, always humbled by His greatness and His love, demonstrating to those around us what it is like to live life knowing that God is in control and that we are His servants.

Every time we allow other things to take over our time and energy, we not only demote God and fail to exalt His name, but we also exchange a God-centred way of life for one which is hedonistic and self-centred. We fall into the trap of exalting ourselves more than God, foolishly putting ourselves first. It is so easy to do: the world encourages it, but we must not allow ourselves to put these "vain idols" first, for it is God whom we must exalt.

The example of David

We see in the life of King David a perfect example of this kind of humility: of someone who truly exalted God above anything else in his life. At the end of his successful reign, he proclaimed before all the people:

> "*Yours*, O LORD, is the greatness and the power and the glory and the victory and the majesty, for all that is in the heavens and in the earth is yours. *Yours* is the kingdom, O LORD, and *you* are exalted as head above all."
>
> (1 Chronicles 29:11)

He could have boasted before the people that all things were under his dominion and that every victory had been down to his perfect leadership. However, he chose to exalt God, not himself. He was not puffed up (the same Hebrew word as "exalted") but he ascribed all of the greatness, power, glory, victory and majesty to God. In verse 14 he acknowledged, "all things come from you, and of your own have we given you". David knew that the kingdom and all that was in it wasn't his to own to rule over: it was given to him by God.

We may not be rulers of a great nation but we are, in a way, rulers of our own lives. We have the free will to do whatever we please, to reject God, to take selfish pride in our achievements, to seek fame and fortune and attribute all this success to ourselves: but what a self-centred attitude this would be! Sadly, it is one we are increasingly encouraged to cultivate and one which we are all guilty of possessing from time to time. Such an attitude raises us up in our estimation. We become proud and self-absorbed, focusing inwards and not upwards. Hosea tells us the end result of this kind of self-satisfied attitude:

> "According to their pasture, so were they filled; they were filled, and their heart was exalted; therefore *they have forgotten me.*" (Hosea 13:6, KJV)

We need to take steps in our lives to ensure it can never be said of us that we have become so proud we have completely forgotten God.

The antidote

What measures can we take, then, to remove such pride from our lives? Moses gave the nation of Israel clear guidelines, in order that they might not forget God in the face of victory, security and abundance. He instructed the people to keep God's commandments –

> "lest, when you have eaten and are full and have built good houses ... and your silver and gold is multiplied ... then your heart be lifted up, and you forget the LORD your God ... Beware lest you say in your heart, 'My power and the might of my hand have gained me this wealth.'" (Deuteronomy 8:11-14,17)

So we are to keep God's commandments, looking to Him for guidance. We must remember that our talents, success, health and wealth come from God, to use in His service and to His glory, never our own. We are not kings and queens of our own lives, no matter what the world tells us; God reigns supreme in our lives and all good things come from Him. We must never become so conceited that we seek our own glory.

God will exalt us

We know that we must never seek to exalt ourselves, but what, then, of the passages where we read that God exalts His people? There are, for example, in the Old Testament a handful of slightly obscure verses which talk about a person's "horn" being exalted. According to *Smith's Bible Dictionary*, the horn was a symbol of strength, honour and victory. As a barren woman, Hannah had experienced shame and ridicule, but when God granted her a child, she declared, "my horn is exalted in the LORD" (1 Samuel 2:1, NKJV). She rejoiced because God had answered her prayer and restored her dignity and honour. Yet even when God lifted her up in this way, she did not become proud, but rather acknowledged that she was exalted "in the LORD". Without Him, she knew she had nothing.

A similar passage is found in Psalm 89, where we read:

> "Blessed are the people who know the festal shout, who walk, O LORD, in the light of your face, who exult in your name all the day and in your righteousness are exalted. For you are the glory of their strength; by your favour our horn is exalted." (verses 15-17)

Like Hannah, the people who chose to exalt God's name and to walk "in the light of [His] face" were exalted in His righteousness and by His favour. God exalts those whom He knows will give *Him* the glory and not seek it for themselves.

The important point to take away here is that *God* chooses who to exalt and does so in order that *He* might ultimately be glorified and exalted, not man. If we are proud, we are not in a position to exalt God (He is all but forgotten) and so He will not see fit to exalt us, choosing rather to humble us so that we might learn to put Him first; but if we are humble and acknowledge that God is our strength, He will exalt us and work great things through us (see Matthew 23:12).

In practical terms, this means that those who put themselves first, boasting in their wealth and success, will not be exalted by God, either in this life or in the kingdom. They have the acclaim of men and women here and now. "They have received their reward" (Matthew 6:2). Solomon certainly understood that this was "vanity and a striving after wind" (Ecclesiastes 2:17), and surely we can see this too.

For the believer who becomes arrogant and fails to put God first, Job has a stark warning: "The LORD gives, and the LORD takes away" (Job 1:21, NET). Parents will sometimes choose to discipline an ungrateful, selfish child by taking away privileges or possessions in order to make them appreciate what they have and learn to be grateful. In asking our Heavenly Father to make us more like Him, we must accept that He may choose to discipline us in a similar way, in order to remove pride and arrogance from our hearts and make us better disciples.

On the other hand, those who have learnt (perhaps the hard way) to put God first, forsaking all that holds them back from doing so, "will receive a hundredfold now in this time ... and in the age to come, eternal life" (Mark 10:30, NKJV). This is not to say that life will be easy, but God promises that, if we seek first *His* kingdom and *His* righteousness, rather than our own goals and our own glory, He will provide all that we need and by His mercy grant us a place in His kingdom.

Exalted in all the earth

The remaining passages in the Old Testament in which God exalts one of His people refer to exalting (or lifting up) kings and leaders. These include Joshua (4:14), David (2 Samuel 22:49), Jeroboam (1 Kings 14:7), Hezekiah (2 Chronicles 32:23) and of course Jesus (Isaiah 52:13). We know from Daniel 4:17 that "the Most High rules the kingdom of men and gives it to whom he will and sets over it the lowliest of men". These men were "chosen from the people" (Psalm 89:19) and God promoted them to positions of authority, in order that His purpose with the earth might be fulfilled.

These kings may have been given authority for a little while, in order that a small part of God's plan could be set in motion, but we look forward to a time when man's pride will be brought low and God will be exalted in all the earth. "The LORD alone will be exalted in that day", declares Isaiah (2:11).

"And you will say in that day: 'Give thanks to the LORD, call upon his name, make known his deeds among the peoples, proclaim that his name is exalted.'" (12:4)

May we all determine to exalt God to the highest place in our lives now, so that we might rejoice on that great and glorious day when God will exalt those whom He has chosen and grant them eternal life in His kingdom.

Questions and suggestions

- Has anything in your life become more important to you than God? This could be your family, career, a hobby or a specific goal. It may also include obsessions (money, body image, finding the right partner) and addictions.
- How might you redress this balance? (Focusing more time on God's word, devoting more time to prayer, reducing the amount of time spent doing a certain hobby, seeking counselling for addictions to reduce their impact in your life and help you regain control.)
- Are you prepared to allow God to work in your life, removing those things which stand between the two of you? Pray for strength to accept His discipline and wise judgement, and be prepared to "let go and let God". He knows what He is doing!

Chapter 6
F for Fellowship

HOW important is your ecclesia to you? Do you look forward to spending time with your brothers and sisters every week? Do you feel a sense of belonging? How well do you know your brothers and sisters, and to what lengths would you go to meet regularly with those who share your faith? These are just some of the questions I would encourage you to ask yourself as you read what follows, and to ponder as you meet with your ecclesial family over the coming weeks.

A matter of priority

For those of us in the UK at least, meeting together every Sunday is something we often take for granted. It is no real hardship to get to the meeting and we don't usually have to travel very far. Most of us have never experienced real isolation and can't truly comprehend just how much of a blessing it is to be able to meet together regularly with our brothers and sisters in Christ. Whenever we catch ourselves taking the gift of fellowship for granted, we need to be mindful of the many brothers and sisters all over the world who meet with other Christadelphians only a handful of times each year. They long to live close to other brothers and sisters and belong to an ecclesia – even a small one – and we must never forget how privileged we are to be able to meet together so easily.

Sometimes, it is simply not possible to get to the meeting on a Sunday: it may be our only possible travel date, or we are looking after someone who is ill; but other times, we are perhaps a little too quick to make plans that interfere with getting to the meeting. Do we really need to drive home from a week's holiday on a Sunday? Could we find an ecclesia to attend en route? Is a child's birthday party really more important to us than attending the breaking of bread? Being a musician, I am sometimes asked to attend rehearsals or play in concerts on a Sunday or on a Bible Class night. Whilst I try always to work around this problem, it can be easy to seek to compromise, rather than to take a firm stand. I'm sure we can all think of similar situations in our own lives: work commitments, sporting events, family gatherings, and any number of other conflicting interests.

We naturally desire to fit in with the people around us and to be part of the various communities in which we live, but we should think carefully about how much affinity we feel with the world. We should always feel more of a sense of belonging to our ecclesia than we do to any other group. If this is not the case, then there are two solutions: either we invest less time and energy in groups outside the ecclesia, or we invest more time and energy in ecclesial activities. We shall consider ways in which we might achieve the latter later in this chapter.

Love one another

We all know the saying, "You can choose your friends, but you can't choose your family". How true this is! Our ecclesial family consists of men, women, children and teenagers of all ages, each having had a different upbringing, with their own perspective on life and unique personality. Were it not for our shared faith, it is likely that you would never have met most of the members of your ecclesia, and would certainly not have developed such a close relationship with them that you would consider them your brothers and sisters. In his first letter to Timothy, Paul writes:

> "Do not rebuke an older man but encourage him as you would a father. Treat younger men like brothers, older women like mothers, younger women like sisters, in all purity." (5:1,2)

He shows us how important it is to love and respect our ecclesial family, as we would our natural family.

Because we all come from different backgrounds, it can be difficult to get along and disagreements often arise, just as they do at home. However, in the same way that we have to make an effort to get along with our natural family, we must do the same with our spiritual family. We should take the time to get to know and understand each other, respecting each other's opinions and "[counting] others more significant than [ourselves]" (Philippians 2:3).

It follows that we should make every effort to avoid doing or saying things that will offend or upset other members of our ecclesia. We should never forge ahead with something about which others have a conscience, just because we ourselves have no problem with it (see 1 Corinthians 8:13).

Role models

To make any family work, teamwork is required. We must all make sure we are pulling our weight and sharing the load. I was talking to a sister recently who belongs to an ecclesia which had a sudden influx of new members from a neighbouring ecclesia. She explained that the new members never came into the kitchen to help with the food preparation or washing up, perhaps because they didn't want to tread on anyone's toes. One Sunday, the sister in question decided that she would simply *not* clear up. In next to no time, the new members began taking things into the kitchen to wash up!

We really are creatures of habit, and once we have established job roles within the ecclesia, we rarely think to change these. However, it is worth bearing in mind that, just because Sister X always cleans the tables after lunch, or Brother Y always locks up after Bible Class, this doesn't mean they wouldn't appreciate a break! Phrases like, "Can I help you with ...?" and "Would you like me to ...?" can be a real tonic to the weary!

Sharing the load like this is just one way in which we can be good role models to the children and teenagers in our ecclesias. We need to cultivate a friendly environment where everyone can feel involved and helpful. Having worked in a primary school for several years, I have always been simultaneously amused and encouraged by the willingness of children to wash up paint pots and paintbrushes, wipe the tables or tidy the cloakroom. Their parents are always incredulous when they are told at Parents' Evening that they have a helpful child who loves tidying, because of course this character trait never manifests itself at home!

If children are so willing to help at school, we should also encourage them to help out at the meeting. Many of them would feel immensely pleased to be given the job of wiping the tables or drying the dishes, especially if they could do this with their friends. Too often, the adults at an ecclesia do all the work without question while the children do their own thing, but a true family will work together and, in doing so, become a stronger family unit.

Another important way in which the divide between young and not-so-young can be broken down – and one which will help children to grow up loving coming to the meeting – is for the adults in an ecclesia to take a genuine interest in the children and teenagers there. Most children easily form bonds with adults who take time to get to know them, and who are interested in what they have to say. The bonds that are formed in this way are important as children become teenagers and perhaps begin to lose interest in the meeting. For them, having good relationships with trustworthy, dependable role models is absolutely crucial. I know several brothers and sisters who would have stopped going to the meeting as teenagers, were it not for a certain brother or sister who just seemed to "get" them and who regularly invited them round to their house and made them feel included.

Actions speak louder …

Of course, it is not just teenagers we should be looking out for. Everyone attending our ecclesias deserves to feel valued and included. We should never forget how difficult it is to be a teenager, but equally we must always be mindful of how exhausting it is to be a parent and how lonely it is to live alone and should never assume that someone is coping, just because they don't ask for help.

Being a parent of young children is no easy task, so offers to babysit, bring round a hot meal, or simply an offer of company (reassuring exhausted mums that it doesn't matter to you that their house is a mess or that they haven't had time to take a shower yet) are appreciated more than we could ever know.

Parents with young children often arrange to meet up during the week, which is great. However, be mindful of those who may feel pushed out – either because they don't have children of their own, or children who are older – and make an effort to invite them to join in with your activities. Not only can they provide sane, non-baby-related conversation, but they can also be a useful extra pair of hands!

Older members of the ecclesia, who perhaps struggle to leave the house, are nevertheless always eager to have visitors round for coffee and a chat. Perhaps you could also offer to do their weekly shop, take the bins out, do some laundry or cook a meal. Whilst they are likely able to do these tasks themselves, they can still be a time-consuming, exhausting burden which they would gladly be rid of once in a while.

I appreciate that most readers will struggle to do any of the above if they work full-time, but why not make a habit of inviting a few members of your ecclesia round for dinner once a month? Doing things outside of the ecclesial setting can really strengthen relationships between brothers and sisters, and changes the atmosphere and dynamic of the ecclesia in a positive way.

It might also be possible to organise regular ecclesial outings and fellowship days where members of the ecclesia (and their families) spend the day together, getting to know each other in a more informal setting. All of these things help us to feel like a real family and greatly increase our sense of belonging.

Talk about what matters

Whether we meet on a Sunday or for coffee during the week, we must always remember the one thing that binds us all together: our faith. The more of an effort we make to talk about the scriptures and about the way God is working in our lives, the better our relationship will be with our brothers and sisters. This might feel strange at first, especially if we are used to talking exclusively about work, family or sport, but it can be so rewarding to find out what another brother or sister is most looking forward to about the kingdom, or to discuss the exhortation and ponder its relevance to our own lives. Talking together about our faith can be a real boost and makes a change from the often mundane conversations we have at other times.

Finally, when we ask a brother or sister how they are, let's *really* ask how they are, taking the time truly to listen. We can break down huge barriers by taking off our 'Sunday mask' and sharing something of our own struggles (even small ones). In doing this, we show others that we are willing to have an honest conversation and admit that we're not as strong as we seem. They may be relieved finally to have someone to share their burden with, and to know that they're not the only one who finds life difficult.

We should want to spend as much time as possible with our brothers and sisters, getting to know them better and growing in faith, away from the pull of the world and its many distractions and temptations. The fellowship we share is a gift from God which we must never take for granted, and one which He has promised we can enjoy together for eternity when His kingdom is established on the earth.

Questions and suggestions

- How important is your ecclesia to you? Do you feel a sense of belonging?
- Do you look forward to spending time with your brothers and sisters every week? Do you take that fellowship for granted?
- How well do you know your brothers and sisters, and to what lengths would you go to meet regularly with those who share your faith?

- How can you be a better role model to the younger members and children at your ecclesia? How can you make sure they feel involved?
- Choose a member of your ecclesia who you know would appreciate some help or company, and make an effort to meet their need. In doing so, you will strengthen your relationship with them.

Chapter 7 — G for Goal

AS we look back on our recent past, we have an opportunity to reflect on the highs and lows of our personal journey of discipleship. What has been our focus? Did we strive to glorify God at all times or did we get distracted along the way? How has our relationship with Him fared? How have we interacted with those around us? Have we held on to the hope of Israel and enthusiastically shared it with others? What impact have recent world events had on us? If Jesus returned today, would we be prepared?

The ultimate goal

Moving forward, what are your spiritual goals and how will you achieve them? How will you stay focused in a world so full of chaos and distraction?

In his letter to the Philippians, the Apostle Paul tells us that his own ultimate spiritual goal is resurrection from the dead. He then sets out the means by which he would attain this (3:9-11):

1. Be found in Christ;
2. Have a righteousness which comes through faith;
3. Know Christ and the power of his resurrection;
4. Share in his sufferings.

How did he put this into practice? It wasn't enough for Paul simply to be "in Christ". He wanted to be "found in Christ" – found to be living the life of someone "in Christ", not lazy or complacent but actively faithful. It also wasn't enough for him simply to "know Christ" as an academic exercise. He knew that, in order truly to know Christ, he had to imitate him and share in his sufferings.

Of course, we all share Paul's ultimate goal. We have been baptized into Christ (Galatians 3:27) and we know the power of his resurrection. Now, like Paul, we must strive to reflect this in our actions, since good works – good fruit – naturally stem from a strong faith (James 2:17; Galatians 5:22,23), while from a true understanding of Christ's death and resurrection comes a willingness to turn our backs on the world, to make meaningful and often difficult sacrifices, and so to share in his sufferings.

Spiritual resolutions

In his New Testament letters, Paul leaves us with a wealth of practical advice to help us put all of this into practice and to continue to bear good fruit. These tips for godly living draw on the spirit of the law and on the character of Christ. Reading them, we learn how Paul strove to be more like Jesus, sharing in his sufferings and imitating his faith.

Whilst by no means exhaustive, the list at the end of this chapter shows a selection of these exhortational points. As you read through the list, hopefully some of these will stand out as areas you would personally like to improve upon in the coming year. Why not write them down and create your own list of spiritual resolutions for the next few months, should the Lord remain away.

Set your goals

Having chosen your spiritual resolutions, you now need to think realistically about how you will achieve these, bearing in mind that the goal can only ever be to *improve*, not perfect, these things.

Set yourself clearly defined short-, medium- and long-term goals and give these deadlines where appropriate. Visualise what it will be like to have achieved each goal (using scriptural examples where possible). For example, if you choose to focus on prayer, your short-term goal might simply be to pray more than you have been doing, your medium-term goal might be to pray three times a day, while your long-term goal would be for prayer to have become second nature, so that it forms an integral part of your day and you are constantly aware of God's presence. You might choose to visualise Daniel, who prayed three times a day without fail; Nehemiah, for whom it was second nature to offer a prayer when put on the spot; or the Lord Jesus, who spent hours every day in prayer and was in constant communication with his Heavenly Father.

Written on our hearts

We all know from experience that, no matter how good our intentions are when we set our New Year's resolutions, we almost always fail to keep them. We become distracted by worldly worries, philosophies and priorities. Temptations arise. We stumble and fall.

Particularly when these are spiritual resolutions, it can be disheartening to know that we have missed the mark, yet we know that in our mortal state, we shall never be free from sin and always make mistakes. We have "the desire to do what is right, but not the ability to carry it out" (Romans 7:18). Thankfully, God knows and understands this, and by His grace and mercy we are justified by our faith rather than our actions (Romans 3:27,28). We therefore do not strive to keep our spiritual resolutions because we believe that they will make us righteous (pursuing a law of works), but we feel compelled to keep our resolutions because God's law is written on our hearts (Romans 2:15) and we "delight in the law of God in [our] inner being" (Romans 7:22). We *want* to do the right thing, even though our fleshly nature so often gets in the way!

God tells us that –

> "the steps of a man are established by the LORD, when he delights in his way; though he fall, he shall not be cast headlong, for the LORD upholds his hand." (Psalm 37:23,24)

If our heart is right with God and our eyes are fixed on Him, He will give us the strength to keep going. He will keep us from utterly falling, help us to learn from our mistakes and to reach our goal.

Press toward the goal

Returning for a moment to Philippians, let us consider what else Paul had to say about his goal:

> "But one thing I do: *forgetting what lies behind and straining forward to what lies ahead*, I press on towards the goal for the prize of the upward call of God in Christ Jesus." (3:13,14)

Paul, of all people, had a past to be ashamed of, yet he refused to dwell on it, focusing instead on the hope of resurrection and eternal life. He set his mind "on things that are above, not on things that are on earth" (Colossians 3:2), knowing that his sins had been "cast ... into the depths of the sea" (Micah 7:19) and removed "as far as the east is from the west" (Psalm 103:12). No matter how many times we miss the mark, we are to consider ourselves "dead to sin and alive to God in Christ Jesus" (Romans 6:11). The power of Christ's resurrection is far stronger than the power of sin and death.

Leaving behind this heavy weight of sin, we are free to "run with endurance the race that is set before us, looking to Jesus, the founder and perfecter of our faith" (Hebrews 12:1,2). We run towards our goal and fix our eyes on Jesus, who waits at the finishing line for us, having already secured our reconciliation and adoption as sons and daughters of God.

For now, we follow the path he laid out for us – the same path that Paul also desired to take – full of resolutions and hurdles, failure and success. It won't be easy, but we know that at the end of it all, those who have run faithfully will receive a crown of righteousness and everlasting life (2 Timothy 4:8; Revelation 2:10).

I will ...

- Not be ashamed of the Gospel (Romans 1:16).
- Not let sin reign in my body (Romans 6:12).
- Delight in God's law in my innermost being (Romans 7:22).
- Not become proud (Romans 11:20).
- Live peaceably with all (Romans 12:18).
- Glorify God in my body (1 Corinthians 6:20).
- Be free from anxieties (1 Corinthians 7:32).

- Exercise self-control in all things (1 Corinthians 9:25).
- Do everything in love (1 Corinthians 16:13).
- Not lose heart when afflicted (2 Corinthians 4:16,17).
- Widen my heart (2 Corinthians 6:13).
- Cleanse body and spirit of defilement (2 Corinthians 7:1).
- Give generously and cheerfully (2 Corinthians 8:2,3; 9:7).
- Be humble, gentle, patient and loving (Ephesians 4:2).
- Forgive others (Ephesians 4:32).
- Be thankful (Ephesians 5:4).
- Count others more significant than myself (Philippians 2:3,4).
- Not grumble (Philippians 2:14,15).
- Rejoice in the Lord always (Philippians 3:1; 4:4).
- Learn to be content in all situations (Philippians 4:11).
- Seek the things that are above (Colossians 3:1).
- Not be angry (Colossians 3:8).
- With thanks do all in the name of Jesus (Colossians 3:17).
- Work heartily as for the Lord, not men (Colossians 3:23).
- Make the best use of time (Colossians 4:5).
- Speak to please God, not man (1 Thessalonians 2:4).
- Control my body in holiness and honour (1 Thessalonians 4:4,5).
- Live quietly, minding my own business (1 Thessalonians 4:11).
- Encourage the faint-hearted; help the weak (1 Thessalonians 5:14).

- Pray without ceasing (1 Thessalonians 5:17).
- Not quarrel, but be kind to everyone (2 Timothy 2:24).
- Patiently reprove, rebuke and exhort (2 Timothy 4:2).
- Be submissive to rulers and authorities (Titus 3:1).
- Speak evil of no one (Titus 3:2).
- Be content, free from love of money (Hebrews 13:5).

Questions and suggestions

- What spiritual resolution(s) will you set yourself? Define a short-, medium- and long-term goal for each resolution.
- Are you ready to handle failure? Recognise that the path of discipleship is a narrow, winding one, full of potholes and other obstacles. Show grace towards yourself, just as God does, and pick yourself up when you fall.
- Do you have your eye on the prize? Keep the vision clear as you run towards that goal!

Chapter 8
H for Humility

IN his parable about the Pharisee and the tax collector (Luke 18:9-14), Jesus contrasts two men who had very different approaches to religion. The Pharisee openly boasted that he had done all that was required of him, whereas the tax collector cast his eyes to the ground, humbly acknowledged his sinfulness and asked God for mercy. The context of this parable is significant. Jesus was speaking to "some who trusted in themselves that they were righteous, and treated others with contempt" (verse 9). In other words, he was speaking to those who, like the Pharisee in the parable, were self-satisfied, self-righteous and who lacked humility. They boasted about their good deeds, refusing to acknowledge a need for repentance and forgiveness, and looked down on those who did not meet their 'high' standards.

Whitewashed tombs

In Matthew's Gospel, Jesus criticised such a hypocritical attitude, saying:

> "Woe to you, scribes and Pharisees, hypocrites! For you are like whitewashed tombs, which outwardly appear beautiful, but within are full of dead people's bones and all uncleanness. So you also outwardly appear righteous to others, but within you are full of hypocrisy and lawlessness."
> (23:27,28)

Jesus knew that their hearts were full of deceit, but others believed the façade and the scribes and Pharisees were held in high standing.

We may not consider ourselves in league with the scribes and Pharisees when it comes to self-righteousness, but how often do we seek to give a good impression? How eager are we to flaunt our godliness and to maintain a good reputation amongst our brothers and sisters? We know that "the heart is deceitful above all things, and desperately wicked" (Jeremiah 17:9, KJV). Our hearts try to convince us that we're inherently good people but, if we use God's word as our guide, we should be only too aware of our sinfulness. How much effort do we put in to cover up this sinfulness in order to appear more righteous than we really are? If our brothers and sisters could read our hearts and our motives, would they see us in a different light, or do we already openly confess our faults and failings, in all humility? Could we too be accused of being like whitewashed tombs?

Such a proud attitude is problematic in many ways. First, if we fail to acknowledge the extent to which we miss the mark, we shall never truly understand the magnitude of Christ's sacrifice, or our need for it. Not only this, but the more highly we think of ourselves, the less humility we demonstrate, and we know that "everyone who exalts himself will be humbled, but the one who humbles himself will be exalted" (Luke 18:14). This lack of humility can also pose a huge stumbling block to our brothers and sisters who see and believe in our outward holiness, unaware of the struggles and flaws just underneath the surface. Without meaning to, we may intensify feelings of inadequacy and isolation in others.

Raising the bar

The Sermon on the Mount eliminates any claim to righteousness we could possibly have. When asked to go one mile, we are exhorted to walk two. When someone asks for the shirt off our back, we are told to give them our coat as well (Matthew 5:40,41). There is always more we could be doing, so we can never sit back and say, 'I have done all that is required of me, therefore I am holy and righteous'.

When it comes to the Ten Commandments, Jesus again raises the bar. Not only does he condemn adultery, but adds that to even look at a woman (or man) "with lustful intent" (verse 28) is to sin. Everyone knew that murder ran contrary to God's law, but Jesus extended this command, saying that we must refrain also from anger and from harbouring resentment and grudges (verse 22).

He finishes by telling us, "You therefore must be *perfect*, as your heavenly Father is perfect" (verse 48), thus raising the bar impossibly high. Surely this is to show us that, without God's grace, we cannot be made righteous.

We must therefore never underestimate the magnitude of Christ's sacrifice, since it is only through the redemptive work of the Lord Jesus Christ that we are reconciled to God. We can do nothing to save ourselves. If we truly understand that God's standards are far higher than anything we can ever achieve, there will be no capacity for self-righteousness. Rather, we shall approach God like the tax collector, in all humility and with thankful hearts, knowing that we deserve death, but that God has granted us life.

Christ in you

As humans, we are rarely altruistic, often selfish and far prouder than we like to admit. Even when we do the right thing, it is often for the wrong reasons, yet we shall only truly appreciate this if we regularly immerse ourselves in the word of God and apply His standards to our lives. We need constantly to compare our thoughts and conduct with the perfect example of the Lord Jesus. Doing this, we become more and more aware of how often we miss the mark, how impossible it is to be like him, and how in need we are of God's grace.

The result of this is godly humility and a desire to do the right thing, even though we know that we shall so often fail. Though we know it is an impossible task, we must nevertheless strive to be like Christ. In doing so, we show that we belong to him and that we desire, like him, to follow the spirit of the law of life, which "has set [us] free … from the law of sin and death" (Romans 8:2).

Drop the façade

Knowing how sinful we are – how deserving of death – we would never claim righteousness before God, rather coming before Him in all humility. Why, then, do we so often cling to our human desire to appear righteous before our brothers and sisters? We have an innate tendency to think too highly of ourselves and too little of others, and this shows in the way we interact with others and conduct our lives. If we become proud of our good works and godly characteristics, bolstered by the well-meaning praise we receive from others, then we are at risk of believing ourselves to be more righteous than we really are, and better than those around us.

There is, of course, nothing wrong with doing good works and displaying godly characteristics, but we need to get the balance right between setting a good example to those around us and openly admitting our human frailty. If we constantly hide behind a mask of spirituality and confidence, we greatly distance ourselves from our brothers and sisters. Putting up too much of a barrier means we come across as intimidating, judgemental and unsympathetic – whether or not that is actually true.

Our brothers and sisters are more likely to trust and confide in us if they know that we have just as many imperfections as they do. We don't need to shout about our deepest, darkest secrets, but simply admitting small faults and struggles can make a big difference, both to us and to those around us. If we begin to let the cracks show, we not only seem more approachable, but we also open ourselves up to receiving support and compassion from our brothers and sisters. Suddenly, our ecclesia starts to feel more like a family and less like a room full of perfect people who make us feel guilty and inadequate about our own flawed discipleship.

The right kind of humility

As with any character trait, it is possible to take humility too far to one extreme. An absence of humility leads to boastfulness and arrogance, but an excess of humility can be just as damaging. It can be only too easy to let humility develop into feelings of inadequacy and inferiority, constantly comparing ourselves to others. Conversely, we may already experience these self-deprecating emotions as a result of our life's circumstances and proudly label them "humility", but humility and low self-esteem are not the same thing.

We realistically know that *no one* is righteous, *no one* is good and *all* fall short of the glory of God, so we need to stop regarding our own fleshly nature as any better or worse than anyone else's. We should only feel inadequate when comparing ourselves to the Lord Jesus Christ and our Heavenly Father. It would be hypocritical of anyone else to make us feel like we are worthless or somehow inferior to them, and we should never purposefully cause any of our brothers or sisters to feel this way about themselves.

The most remarkable thing is that God, who above all others would have every reason to make us feel inferior and to look down on us with contempt, tells us again and again that He loves us. He does not treat us the way we deserve to be treated, but instead tells us that we are worthy, "not because of our works but because of his own purpose and grace" (2 Timothy 1:9).

We know that the very hairs of our head are numbered, and that we are of more value to Him than many sparrows (Luke 12:7). God tells us that we are precious in His eyes, and honoured, and that He loves us (Isaiah 43:4), and we know that nothing can separate us from His love (Romans 8:39). "He ... did not spare his own Son but gave him up for us all" (verse 32). Our robes have been washed clean by the blood of the Lamb (Revelation 7:14), and our transgressions have been removed as far as the east is from the west (Psalm 103:12), so that it can be said of us – the bride of Christ – "You are altogether beautiful, my love; there is no flaw in you" (Song of Solomon 4:7). What other response would suffice, except to bow before our Heavenly Father with utmost thanks, reverence and humility?

Questions and suggestions

- Do your brothers and sisters in Christ always see a true reflection of your heart and mind, or do you sometimes hide behind a façade of confidence, happiness and spiritual zeal?

- Consider how such a façade could be a stumbling block to your brothers and sisters.
- Are you approachable or do you seem too 'sorted'?
- How might you go about developing more frank, open relationships with those around you?

Chapter 9
J for Integrity

JOB, David and others were commended for their integrity (Job 2:3; 1 Kings 9:4, Genesis 20:6) and the writers of the Psalms and Proverbs in particular place great emphasis on the importance of this characteristic, but what is godly integrity, and how do we develop it?

Structurally sound

A building is said to have structural integrity if it will not bend, break or collapse under its own weight, or the weight of any load it is required to bear. A structurally sound building is designed so that, even if one part is damaged, it does not lead to an entire collapse. In the same way, a person shows integrity if their faith and values do not waver or buckle under pressure. It is an outward demonstration of faith and steadfastness when faced with trials and temptation. Within our ecclesias and wider community, we should be supporting each other so that if one brother's or sister's faith is shaken, those around them form a network of support and help restore their faith.

Faithful examples

When he heard that King Darius had forbidden the worship of anyone or anything but himself, Daniel's faith was not shaken. He refused to let external pressures influence the way he worshipped God, or prevent him from doing the right thing. Daniel did not presume that God would save him – though he certainly believed that He could – but continued to pray at his open window three times a day, knowing that the consequence of doing so was death. His resolve was firm and he was determined to serve God and not man. Daniel's integrity was rewarded by God. First, he was saved from the mouths of lions, but more importantly, he is listed in Hebrews 11 as a man of faith who will inherit the kingdom of God.

We may not be faced with a den of lions or presidents plotting our demise, but we are often faced with external pressures that question our integrity. How often does our desire to fit in with those around us tempt us to compromise our integrity and morals? Do we pause a conversation in the staff room or office in order to give thanks before lunch, or are we embarrassed to draw attention to our faith? Are we honest and thorough in every aspect of our work, honouring our earthly masters, or are we tempted to cut corners? Do we break copyright and traffic laws because others do and we think we can get away with it? There are so many opportunities to demonstrate our faith, to preach the Gospel, and to serve God, but we miss so many of them because we care too much about what the world expects and don't want to appear unusual or overly zealous. We want to fit in.

Our integrity is put to the test in the face of intense trials: the death of a loved one; failing health; financial struggles; the emotional and physical impact of war, terrorism and crime; the pain of rejection. All these can have such a bearing on our emotional and spiritual well-being that we may question our faith, doubt God's love or even His existence, and say or do things that are not right. Job knew what it was like to lose loved ones, to suffer great pain, to be rejected by others, and to lose everything. The emotional trauma he experienced must have been crippling, yet he held on to his faith. He refused to "curse God and die" (Job 2:9) and was commended for being a blameless and upright man who held fast his integrity in spite of adversity (verse 3). Can the same be said of you and me?

Building a wall

Our faith is like a wall, each brick uniquely crafted from experience. If we spend time getting to know and understand God's values, our bricks will be fashioned from the fruit of the Spirit and will be held together by a desire to love God and each other. The more time we spend with God's word, surrounded by those who desire to live in ways that please Him, the stronger our wall will become. Conversely, if we spend our time in the wrong company, absorbing bad morals and ungodly thinking, our bricks will be made of these things. Our wall may be strong, but it will not be pleasing to God. We know from the parable of the wise and foolish men that unless we build on the rock of God, our wall cannot stand. The Psalmist writes, "He alone is my rock and my salvation, my fortress; I shall not be greatly shaken" (Psalm 62:2).

Defending our wall

We may feel that we are building a strong wall of faith, with God as our firm foundation, but even the strongest walls can crumble in a storm or be torn down in battle. How prepared are we to defend our wall? How will we repair any broken sections? How can we strengthen our defences so that our integrity is not compromised?

Consider Nehemiah and his men, whose sole concern for many days was to build a physical wall around Jerusalem. They were under constant pressure from those around them to stop building, and endured ridicule which threatened to destroy their morale. Sanballat and Tobiah, along with the Arabs, the Ammonites and the Ashdodites, plotted against Jerusalem to prevent the wall from being rebuilt (Nehemiah 4:7,8).

It comes as no surprise that Nehemiah's first response was to pray (verse 9). He then set up a guard, stationing the people along the wall, clan by clan, armed and ready to defend (verse 13). Finally, he reassured the people, saying, "Do not be afraid of them. Remember the Lord, who is great and awesome … Our God will fight for us" (verses 14,20).

We see a strong parallel between the wall they were building, and our own wall of faith. Taunts and pressures, trials and temptations are inevitable, and so we must be prepared to defend that which we are building. Our first line of defence is prayer. God wants us to succeed in growing our faith and will help us to do so, if we ask Him. Sometimes, though, the best way for our faith to grow is for us to weather the storm and fight the battle, for we know that the genuineness of our faith – its integrity – will be tested by various trials (1 Peter 1:6) so that we "may be perfect and complete, lacking in nothing" (James 1:4). In these circumstances, we must make sure we are able to defend our faith, both internally (against hopelessness, doubt and other emotions) and externally (against peer pressure and worldly standards).

The whole armour of God

Paul tells us that we defend our faith by taking up –

> "the whole armour of God, that you may be able to withstand in the evil day, and having done all, to stand firm.

Stand therefore, having fastened on the *belt of truth*, and having put on the *breastplate of righteousness*, and, as shoes for your feet, having put on the *readiness given by the gospel of peace*. In all circumstances take up the *shield of faith*, with which you can extinguish all the flaming darts of the evil one; and take the *helmet of salvation*, and the *sword of the Spirit*, which is the word of God." (Ephesians 6:13-17)

I encourage you to consider how each element applies to your own life, and to think about any pieces of your armour which might require repair. No soldier would choose to go into battle with parts of his armour missing or damaged. Why should we treat our own armour any differently? How will we stand upright, retaining and defending our integrity in the face of trials, if we have not kept our spiritual armour well-oiled? Our God will fight for us, but we have to do our part.

Working together

When Nehemiah set a guard over the wall of Jerusalem, he stationed the people in clans or families, each defending a different part. Half of them worked while the other half stood guard (Nehemiah 4:16).

God has set us in families, or ecclesias, for the same purpose of working together to build and defend. Each priest repaired the section of wall opposite his house (3:28). Each had their own part to build, and together these formed a much larger wall.

We, too, are building something greater than our own small wall. Our lives and faith are connected with those of our brothers and sisters.

Structural engineers have to ensure that a building will not collapse when one part of it is damaged. If you have ever played the game Jenga you will know that to remove a block from the bottom results in collapse – the bricks above have nothing to support them. However, if the tower is a little wider, constructed of interlocking bricks, it remains upright even if a block is removed from the bottom, since the bricks above the hole are supported by those on either side. The wider the construction, the greater its capacity to hold together and the better its structural integrity.

So it is, that by building together we support each other when trials strike heavy blows and temptations eat away at our faith. On our own we might collapse, but with the support of our brothers and sisters we can bear them.

When cracks and holes do appear in our wall, as inevitably they will, this need not herald the destruction of our faith and integrity. We all make mistakes that we later regret. Peter denied Christ, even though he was adamant that he never would. David committed adultery and engineered the death of an innocent man, then spent months in denial.

When times like these arise, we should not lose heart. Instead, let these moments of weakness serve to remind us that we need continually to dig deep into God's word, to make new and stronger bricks, and to oil our armour so that we are better ready to defend our faith in future; and when we see our brother or sister struggling to repair their own wall, we should support them, read with them, pray with them and for them, and help them to rebuild that which has been broken.

At the end of it all, having endured all manner of trials and temptations, and having had our integrity tested to the limit, may we all be able faithfully to say:

"I have walked in my integrity, and I have trusted in the LORD without wavering." (Psalm 26:1)

Questions and suggestions

- Can you think of a time recently when your integrity was put to the test? How did you fare? Could you have acted differently?
- Has a desire to conform ever caused you to compromise your integrity?
- Do you show integrity in the small things?
- Is your armour in good repair? What one thing could you do this week to strengthen your spiritual integrity?
- Is there someone who you know is struggling to maintain integrity and to remain strong under pressure? How can you support them?

Chapter 10 — J for Joy

OUR capacity for joy is a gift from God. Not only does it drastically improve our quality of life, it also serves as a witness to others of God's goodness: an outward display of the amazing joy God's law brings into the lives of those who keep it. There are so many reasons to be joyful, yet the joy we experience now is nothing compared to that of the saints in the kingdom. In this article, we consider how joy affects every aspect of a disciple's life, and look ahead to the abundant and everlasting joy God has promised to all who hope in Him.

Rejoice in the good

The principle of rejoicing is set out clearly in the book of Deuteronomy, where the Children of Israel are exhorted to rejoice before the Lord their God in all that they do (Deuteronomy 12:7,18). Whether eating, drinking, tithing, offering sacrifices or feasting, they were to be joyful. This is epitomised in chapter 26: "And you shall rejoice in *all the good* that the LORD your God has given to you and to your house" (verse 11). We know that we have an all-powerful God, "who richly provides us with everything to enjoy" (1 Timothy 6:17), and thankfulness and joy are a necessary part of discipleship – a natural response to all the blessings we have received from God.

The Children of Israel were instructed to rejoice together during their many appointed feast times, but expressions of joy should not be restricted to times of feasting and plenty. In 1 Thessalonians 5:16 we read these two simple words: "Rejoice always." *Joy is a way of life.* We can train ourselves to remain joyful even in the most difficult circumstances, since our joy is rooted not in earthly things, which are unstable and fleeting, but in an unchanging, unshakeable God: for "the joy of the LORD is [our] strength" (Nehemiah 8:10).

We can begin by learning to appreciate and enjoy the little things. Life in the modern world is hectic: we are always in a hurry to get somewhere or in a rush to get something done. It seems we have forgotten how to be still. We fail to notice the millions of remarkable things happening right in front of our eyes, from the feel of our own heartbeat and the coolness of inhaled air hitting the back of our throat to the rustle of a gentle breeze or the patter of raindrops. Sometimes, we need to force ourselves to stop thinking and analysing, and simply appreciate what is happening right now. When we do this, we can't fail to see God at work. The peace and contentment we experience in these precious moments lead to a deeper and more lasting kind of joy than the world could ever offer.

Rejoice in your work

"There is nothing better", we read in Ecclesiastes, "than that a man should rejoice in his work, for that is his lot" (Ecclesiastes 3:22). Sometimes, work can be a trial of patience and endurance, be it in the office, at home or in the ecclesia. It is not easy to feel joy when filing tax returns, dealing with irate customers or unloading the washing machine for the third time in one day. However, we are told that all work is a gift from God (5:19).

Joy and thankfulness often go hand in hand, so if we can feel thankful about our work, then we shall instinctively find ourselves rejoicing in it. The fact that we have tax returns to file or customers to deal with (whether our own, or someone else's) means we have been blessed with a job and therefore have a source of income; the fact that we have washing to do means that we not only have clothes and bed linen, but enough money to afford a washing machine and the electricity necessary to run it.

Something I have experienced a lot in the workplace is a misplaced sort of joy. So many people take great pleasure in moaning, complaining and venting their frustration. In our dissatisfied culture, everyone is always striving for bigger, better, more. We are always looking for someone to blame, something to complain about and reasons to moan and groan. We enjoy it!

It is very easy to be swept along by this tide of ungratefulness and discontent which focuses on negativity and stifles joy, but we are exhorted to rise above this kind of thinking. We are to "obey [our] earthly masters ... with a sincere heart" (Ephesians 6:5), to "be content with [our] wages" (Luke 3:14), and accept "weaknesses, insults, hardships, persecutions, and calamities" (2 Corinthians 12:10). There is no room for grumbling in the life of a disciple; rather, we should be content in all situations (Philippians 4:11). Such contentment brings peace and joy into our lives as we focus less energy on the things we cannot change, and devote more time to being grateful for what we have.

What's more, our optimistic attitude and refusal to grumble or be unkind are important if we are to shine God's light into the world. We would be poor ambassadors of God's joyful message of salvation if we were always grumpy and miserable! Our joyful attitude may well serve as a springboard to conversations about our faith. When asked why we never complain about policies, groan about unpaid overtime or go on strike, we can talk about the lasting joy we have found in Christ and about our desire to be more like him.

Most importantly, since we know that all things come from God, a thankful attitude will always make us think about Him throughout the day. It is easy to see why such a mindset is vital to develop if we are to be faithful disciples.

Rejoice in suffering

Perhaps we can easily get to grips with finding joy in the work we have been given to do, but what about rejoicing in our sufferings? Do we find that as easy? Peter gives us some wise insight:

> "Beloved, do not be surprised at the fiery trial when it comes upon you to test you, as though something strange were happening to you. But rejoice insofar as you share Christ's sufferings, that you may also rejoice and be glad when his glory is revealed." (1 Peter 4:12,13)

Though Peter may have been talking specifically about suffering persecution at the hands of unbelievers, the principle can readily be applied to any trials and suffering we might encounter. We should not see our suffering as anything unusual or unique, for we know that there is "nothing new under the sun" (Ecclesiastes 1:9). Instead, we are encouraged to rejoice because it is only through our own suffering that we can hope to comprehend even to a very limited extent that which Christ endured.

In times of suffering, we can look to the perfect example of the Lord Jesus Christ, whose deepest desire was that his joy might be in us, and that our joy might be full (John 15:11). For our sakes, he experienced loneliness, pain and rejection beyond measure, and "for the joy that was set before him endured the cross, despising the shame" (Hebrews 12:2). If Jesus was prepared to endure such suffering, we too must be prepared to share in this, in order that we "may also rejoice and be glad when his glory is revealed" (1 Peter 4:13).

How did Jesus find joy in the darkest places? Take a look at any Messianic Psalm (18, 22, 31, 41 are good examples) and you will notice three things: first, he was not afraid to cry out to God and to pour out his sorrow before Him. Secondly, he acknowledged God's power and goodness, choosing to put his life into the hands of the only one who could save him; and finally, he always looked beyond his present suffering to the promised joy that lay ahead. If we strive to do the same, we can know joy even when circumstances dictate that we should be feeling only despair and hopelessness.

Rejoice in God's word

Do you open your Bible regularly, with anticipation and longing, or do you put off reading it, regarding Bible reading as a chore and an inordinate effort? Do you feel agitated when you haven't spent enough time reading your Bible, or do you feel more frustrated when you miss the latest episode of a favourite TV programme? However you feel, we know that the correct attitude towards God's word is to receive it with joy and gladness, to drink deeply from the well of living water, and to tell those around us of the wonderful things we have read. We should long for God's presence through His word "as a deer pants for flowing streams" (Psalm 42:1).

God's word is like a precious pearl or a priceless treasure and we should find great joy in reading it because it is through its pages that we draw near to God and learn more about His love. "I rejoice at your word", writes the Psalmist, "like one who finds great spoil" (Psalm 119:162). If we don't yet feel this joy, perhaps we need to take a different approach to Bible reading, looking deeper into the pages of scripture, asking *why* an event happened, *why* someone did what they did, rather than just skim-reading to find out *what* happened. We can use resources such as Bible Reading Discussion Cards to help us get more out of the readings.[1] Above all, we must seek to apply the word to our own lives, taking what we read deep into our hearts so that the word of Christ dwells in us richly (Colossians 3:16).

Rejoice in God's salvation

What greater reason is there to rejoice than because of God's salvation? Our Father's love for us is such that He provided a Lamb who would "take away the sin of the world" (John 1:29) and "appear a second time ... to save those who are eagerly waiting for him" (Hebrews 9:28). Even though the world outside our windows is self-destructing, we can rejoice in the hope of God's glory (Romans 5:2), taking joy in Him who clothes us with garments of salvation (Isaiah 61:10), and rejoicing that our names are written in heaven (Luke 10:20).

This joy is not ours alone. It is amazing to read that there is joy in heaven over our repentance (Luke 15:6,7) and that, just as we rejoice in His salvation, so God too rejoices over us "as the bridegroom rejoices over the bride" (Isaiah 62:5). What a beautiful picture!

Rejoice in Jerusalem

Scripture tells us a lot about the joy which we shall all, by God's grace, share in Jerusalem. In Isaiah, we read:

---

[1] These provide a useful stimulus to Bible study (available from the Christadelphian Office).

"For behold, I create new heavens and a new earth, and the former things shall not be remembered or come into mind. But be glad and rejoice forever in that which I create; for behold, I create Jerusalem to be a joy, and her people to be a gladness. I will rejoice in Jerusalem and be glad in my people; no more shall be heard in it the sound of weeping and the cry of distress." (Isaiah 65:17-19)

After thousands of years of war and oppression, Jerusalem will finally be filled with joy, and its people will dwell securely. Mount Zion will be called the joy of the whole earth, the city of the great King (Psalm 48:2) and God will dwell among His people (Zechariah 2:10). We shall see Eden restored.

"The desert shall rejoice and blossom like the crocus; it shall blossom abundantly and rejoice with joy and singing." (Isaiah 35:1,2)

In those latter days, the Children of Zion will again rejoice in their King (Psalm 149:2) and the nations will go up to Jerusalem, to the mountain of the house of the Lord, to hear the word of God (Isaiah 2:2,3). At last, we His saints will come to Jerusalem, our hearts overflowing with gladness, and enter the joy of our Lord (Isaiah 35:10; Matthew 25:21).

Questions and suggestions

- Are you joyful at work / school? Does your cheerful attitude make you stand out from the crowd?
- What are you struggling with right now? How might an attitude of joy and thankfulness change your perspective and help you to find pleasure in life, even in times of trial?

- Take time to enjoy the little things. Smell every rose you walk by; turn your face to the rain and smile; enjoy every breath you take. Be present in the moment and be open to experiencing joy in all things.

Chapter 11
K for Know the Lord

IT is a beautiful thing that the Lord God desires a relationship with us and that He knows us so well. We read in Psalm 139 that He knows where we are, what we are thinking and every word we speak (verses 2,3). Moses was assured that God knew him by name (Exodus 33:17) and in Acts we read that He knows "the hearts of all" (1:24). Such an intimate relationship is not one-sided, but requires that we in turn seek to know our Father, just as He knows us. This is possibly the most important aspect of our discipleship, since we cannot truly imitate, follow and obey God if we do not first know who He is and what He is like.

The Lord our God is one

The most fundamental tenet of our faith is a recognition that "the LORD our God, the LORD is one" (Deuteronomy 6:4) and besides Him, there is no God and no saviour (Isaiah 45:5; Hosea 13:4). We must steer clear of the humanistic thinking of the modern world which tells us that we are our own 'number one' and encourages us to worship material wealth and possessions. There can only be one God in our lives.

> "Before [Him] no god was formed, nor shall there be any after [Him]." (Isaiah 43:10)

He is all-powerful (verse 13) and by His power the earth was created and is sustained. The whole earth and all of its inhabitants – past, present and future – belong to Him (Psalm 24:1).

God does not expect us to believe in Him blindly. Along with ample evidence in creation and world history to prove His existence, a knowledge and appreciation of His character and His power is garnered from our own experience and the well-documented experiences of those who have gone before us.

Interestingly, a knowledge of the Lord is often qualified in scripture by the words 'then' or 'that'. God promised to provide food for the Children of Israel, saying, "*then* you shall know that I am the LORD your God" (Exodus 16:12). He established the Sabbath as a sign between God and man, "*that* you may know that I, the LORD, sanctify you" (31:13). God performed signs and wonders, fighting on Israel's side and bringing them out of Egypt, "*that* [they] might know that the LORD is God; there is no other besides him" (Deuteronomy 4:35). In the same way, God is powerfully working in our lives *that* we might know that He is the Lord, He is in control, and with Him all things are possible (Matthew 19:26).

This is eternal life

Jesus' powerful declaration in John 17 shows us just how important it is to know God:

> "And *this is eternal life*, that they know you the only true God, and Jesus Christ whom you have sent." (verse 3)

Yet it is not enough merely to *say* that we believe in God and know what He is like. Titus warns of those who "profess to know God, but ... deny him by their works" (1:16). The knowledge that we have must lead to action. We must strive to imitate God and the Lord Jesus Christ in all that we do, putting into practice everything we know.

And there is *so much* that we do know! Scripture tells us that God is merciful, gracious, slow to anger, faithful, loving and forgiving (Exodus 34:6,7). The Bible abounds with passages that show what this means in practice. All of these characteristics are evident throughout God's dealings with mankind in both the Old and New Testaments. We also have the perfect example of the Lord Jesus Christ, who shows us that it is possible for a human being to apply godly characteristics in life. He demonstrated to us how to go beyond mere head knowledge and to show God's love in everything we do. It is this demonstration of love that is so important because we are told that *"God is love"* and that "anyone who does not love does not know God" (1 John 4:8). The opposite must therefore also be true: *anyone who shows this love knows God.*

The world does not know

"The reason why the world does not know us", writes John, "is that it did not know him" (1 John 3:1). It can be hard to live in an age and a culture that has no time for God and doesn't understand faith, hope and a godly perspective on life. We may find ourselves criticised, mocked or discriminated against because of our beliefs and attitude to life, but we know that this is nothing new.

The Lord Jesus experienced rejection, scorn and abuse because he stood up for God's ways, showed remarkable integrity and quietly turned the other cheek. In spite of all this,

Jesus chose to forgive those who wronged him. They did so in their ignorance, for they did not know who he really was and they had lost sight of who God was. We too must be willing to forgive those who ridicule our faith and we must also be prepared to accept persecution and hardship for the sake of the Gospel. If the world did not know Jesus two thousand years ago, why should we expect things to be any different now?

Surely we have a responsibility to do everything we can to teach those we come into contact with about God. They do not know Him, but we do. We know without a shadow of a doubt that God exists and that He rewards those who seek Him with eternal life (Hebrews 11:6; Romans 6:23). God "has shone in our hearts to give the light of the knowledge of the glory of God in the face of Jesus Christ" (2 Corinthians 4:6). We are the light of the world, a city on a hill (Matthew 5:14). This is our God-given light, and we ought to shine it into the world with all our might.

Test everything

We must not, however, expect that the world will want to listen. In Exodus 5:2, Pharaoh stated emphatically, "I do not know the LORD". Along with most of the Gentile population, He had no interest in seeking the one true God.

Sadly, such an attitude is reflected by many in the world today. Even those who do profess to know God and the Lord Jesus have largely lost sight of what the Bible teaches. They have their own ideas about the nature and character of God and rely heavily on the traditions of men. Such corruption of knowledge is not new. By the time of Malachi, even those who should have been spiritual leaders had lost sight of who God really was. The priests had become corrupt and were apparently oblivious to the fact that they were no longer serving or pleasing God with their tainted rituals.

We might not be like Pharaoh, utterly denying the existence of God, but perhaps we sometimes share the attitude of the priests. They once knew God and His laws, but somewhere along the way they stopped referring back to the Law of Moses and instead relied on their own writings, new and 'improved' rituals and man-made traditions.

How much do you and I rely on second- or third-hand information about God? How much importance do we place on traditions which, while probably harmless, are man-made and not founded on scripture? Unless we seek guidance directly from scripture, how do we know that the God we worship is the God of the Bible? It is extremely important that we read the scriptures thoroughly, regularly and purposefully, testing everything we hear, read or think to see whether it matches up with what the Bible says (1 Thessalonians 5:21).

A twenty-first century warning

Even if we base our knowledge of God entirely on what we read in the Bible (and hopefully we all do), there is still the very real danger that we are reading with a strong twenty-first century bias. Today's world is obsessed with unity, equality, peace, war, political correctness, animal rights, human rights and self-promotion, to name just a few issues. Morals are important, but are our own morals based on what we know about the world, or what we know about God?

The One we serve is the same God who commanded that whole nations should be destroyed (e.g., 1 Samuel 15:3). He required regular animal sacrifice and may reinstitute this in the kingdom age. He expects men and women to undertake different roles and will not tolerate same-sex relationships. These aspects of God's character are widely at odds with the generally accepted world view in Western society. Even some Christians reject 'the God of the Old Testament' because He seems too harsh and brutal. They seek to put a timeless God into a twenty-first century mould. This is something we must strive to avoid.

When we open the pages of scripture, we must endeavour to cast off all cultural and social bias. We must never approach Bible study with a view to proving our own theory of who God is and what He is like, but must always come with an open mind and heart, desiring to know what the Bible really says about Him. This is the only way we can truly come to know God.

"They shall all know"

Of course, even with the greatest determination and the most devoted Bible study, we know that we cannot yet fully grasp God's character and might. Job proclaimed, "Behold, God is great, and *we know him not*" (36:26). Like Job, we marvel at the wonders of creation and tremble at God's awesome power. There is so much about Him that is beyond our current comprehension, but we look forward to a time when our understanding will be complete.

> "For now we see in a mirror dimly, but then face to face. Now I know in part; then I shall know fully, even as I have been fully known." (1 Corinthians 13:12)

Clothed in immortality and given wisdom and understanding when Christ returns, we shall then truly know the Lord. What is more, in those days God will give stubborn Israel a heart to know that He is the Lord, and they will return to Him (Jeremiah 24:6,7).

> "This is the covenant that I make with the house of Israel after those days, declares the LORD: I will put my law within them, and I will write it on their hearts. And I will be their God, and they shall be my people. And no longer shall each one teach his neighbour and each his brother, saying, 'Know

the LORD', for *they shall all know me*, from the least of them to the greatest, declares the LORD." (31:33,34)

Not only Israel, but all nations will be given the opportunity to learn God's ways and accept His salvation. Many will seek to know God, saying:

"Come, let us go up to the mountain of the LORD, to the house of the God of Jacob, that He may teach us his ways and that we may walk in his paths." (Isaiah 2:3)

It is our firm hope that we shall be there on that day; that we shall be kings and priests with Christ, teaching the nations God's law and helping all to come to a knowledge and understanding of who He is and what He asks of us. At last, the words of Habakkuk's prophecy will have come to pass:

"For the earth will be filled with the knowledge of the glory of the LORD as the waters cover the sea." (Habakkuk 2:14)

Until that time, let us resolve to share God's promises with everyone we meet, so that they too might know the Lord, for "this is eternal life" (John 17:3).

Questions and suggestions

- Do you know God?
- Do you really?
- Do you have a tendency to believe the things you read or hear, so long as they don't sound too far-fetched and you deem the source a credible one? Is this wise?
- In what ways might your view of God be influenced by your culture, modern society and the media?
- How could you help others to come to know God?

Chapter 12
L for Loyalty

IN this chapter I had intended to write about love, having been thinking about God's love for us, and how we are to manifest that same love in our own lives. I considered how, when we truly love someone, we put them first and desire to spend time with them. Wanting to get to the heart of what love is all about, I looked at chapters like 1 Corinthians 13 which tell us so much about love, yet there was one passage that I kept coming back to. It talks about God's love for Israel.

> "For you are a people holy to the LORD your God. The LORD your God has chosen you to be a people for his treasured possession, out of all the peoples who are on the face of the earth. It was not because you were more in number than any other people that the LORD set his love on you and chose you, for you were the fewest of all peoples, but it is because the LORD loves you and is keeping the oath that He swore to your fathers ..." (Deuteronomy 7:6-8)

God's love for Israel is based on a covenant promise, on an oath that cannot be broken. Today, we might call this kind of love 'loyalty' or 'faithfulness'. As we consider several passages in more detail, we shall note how love, loyalty and covenant promises go hand in hand.

Undeserved loyalty

God's loyalty to us has been in existence from the foundation of the world. "In love he *predestined* us for adoption as sons through Jesus Christ, according to the purpose of His will" (Ephesians 1:4,5) and "those whom he *predestined* he also *called*, and those whom he *called* he also *justified*, and those whom he *justified* he also *glorified*" (Romans 8:30).

We know that God sees the end from the beginning and is true to His word. Having predestined us for adoption, we can have confidence that God will remain loyal to those whom He has chosen and will not break His covenant with them.

Abram was one such individual. In Genesis 12, God called Abram out of Ur and made a covenant with him, promising that he would father a great nation and that his offspring would inherit the land of Canaan (verses 2,7). Having grown up at a time when Noah and each of his descendants were still alive, Abram would have known first-hand about God's great power and mercy, yet there is no mention of his faith up until this point. In fact, God's promise appears to come out of nowhere. God had chosen Abram and predestined that he would father a great nation. God would justify him and glorify him not because of Abram's righteousness, but because it was God's will and purpose to do so.

Such a display of undeserved love and loyalty towards a God-fearing yet sinful man of course required a response, and Abram's faithful response pleased God. He believed the promises God made to him, and this was counted to him as righteousness (Genesis 15:6).

A mutual covenant

Twenty-four years after God made His first covenant with Abram, He made another important promise. This time, the covenant was not *with* Abram, but *between* God and Abram. As a result, there were conditions: "I am God Almighty; *walk before me, and be blameless*, that I may make my covenant *between me and you*, and may multiply you greatly" (17:1,2). Abram and his descendants were required to remain loyal to God, walking before Him and obeying His voice, while God promised that He would remain loyal to Abram and his descendants, blessing them and bringing them into the land.

Curiously, it is only now that God changes Abram's name from Abram (exalted father) to Abraham (father of a multitude), even though more than two decades have passed since God first promised that Abram would father a great nation. Surely it is no coincidence that this name change is recorded just before God reveals to Abraham that Sarah would bear a son the following year (verse 21). That which God had promised was now coming to pass and Abraham's name was firstly a testimony to the loyalty and faithfulness of God, who always keeps His promises, and secondly a reminder of the conditions of the covenant he had entered into with God.

Circumcise your heart

From the outset, the covenant had been one of separation. Abraham was called out of Ur, called to be separate and holy to the Lord. Now God required a physical sign of this everlasting covenant. Every male of Abraham's household was to be circumcised and anyone who remained uncircumcised was deemed to have broken the covenant (verses 9-14).

We know that the physical circumcision itself was not what mattered to God, but that it was symbolic of a deeper severance which Abraham and his descendants were to undergo: they were to circumcise themselves to God, removing the foreskin of their hearts (Jeremiah 4:4), to the end that they would love the Lord their God with all their heart and soul, and live (Deuteronomy 30:6). This required them to hold fast to God and put off all idolatrous practices (13:4,6-10). Nothing was to take God's place in their lives.

This, then, was Abraham's side of the covenant, which he and his children were required to keep throughout their generations. As heirs to the same covenant, we too must circumcise our hearts, removing anything that is preventing us from giving our whole heart to God. This might be work commitments, hobbies, material possessions, worries or doubts. God does not ask us to perform great deeds: He just asks for our loyalty and our love. God asks us to seek and to serve Him faithfully, with an undivided heart.

Bound together

Under the same bond of the covenant, we must seek not only to remain steadfastly loyal to God, but also to our brothers and sisters in Christ. At our baptism, we each entered into a binding covenant relationship with our Heavenly Father and became part of a worldwide fellowship of believers. We are bound together in love, which comes from God, and share a vision of a glorious future when we shall inherit the land first promised to Abraham.

Being loyal to our brothers and sisters means putting their needs before our own. It means forgiving them when they do something to annoy or upset us, because their fellowship should mean more to us than our own pride. It means reaching out to those who are struggling, bearing one another's burdens and supporting each other in the face of adversity and opposition. It means that we encourage rather than side-line those whose attendance at meetings is infrequent or reluctant, and we seek to mend damaged relationships before feelings of bitterness or resentment have time to fester. Loyalty to our brothers and sisters must always be a stronger force in our lives than that of our own needs and desires.

Beyond the individual relationships we share, we must also consider how loyal we are being to our ecclesia. Do we honour ecclesial commitments with the same level of loyalty as work commitments? Do we consider how our choices and our actions will impact the ecclesia, or do we think only of our family and our personal spiritual well-being? Do we feel more loyal to friends outside the Truth, or inside? Where do your loyalties lie? Where do mine?

Loyalty in marriage

Ask any married couple and they will tell you that one of the keys to a happy, secure marriage is loyalty. It is an essential characteristic for both husband and wife, if they are to enjoy a successful marriage. Just as God makes a covenant with us, so the bride and groom make a covenant with each other. They promise to remain faithful to each other in all circumstances. Even if a relationship seems for a time to be devoid of all positive emotion and everything seems to be going wrong, a couple's loyalty to each other's emotional happiness and spiritual welfare can be enough to heal rifts and restore a broken relationship. Like a muscle, a bond of commitment and loyalty is something which grows stronger the more it is exercised; the more it is put to the test, the stronger it becomes.

There will be times in any marriage where mistakes are made or misunderstandings arise. Forgiveness might seem impossible and completely undeserved. It is at these times, more than any other, that loyalty is important: loyalty to each other and to the vows (the covenant) made between husband and wife. The Lord God has set us the perfect example to follow. He does not love and forgive us because we deserve it, but because He promised to love us, and will never break this oath. He is fiercely loyal to us.

> "I have loved you with an everlasting love; *therefore* I have continued my faithfulness to you." (Jeremiah 31:3)

Whatever our marital status, we know that each one of us has been called to share the marriage supper of the Lamb, to be part of the bride of Christ. In the Old Testament, God speaks of Israel several times as His beloved bride. "I remember the devotion of your youth, your love as a bride" He proclaims (Jeremiah 2:2), and yet Israel went whoring after the gods of the surrounding nations. They had forgotten their first love.

> "Can a virgin forget her ornaments, or a bride her attire? Yet my people have forgotten me days without number."
> (verse 32)

Though God had remained loyal to His chosen people, continuing in steadfast love towards them, they had rejected Him, despising the oath and breaking the covenant (Ezekiel 16:59). Israel determined that, since they were free and no longer in captivity, they did not need to serve anyone, including God. This kind of attitude is just as prevalent today as it was in Jeremiah's day. People believe that they are free to do as they please. They do not want to serve or obey anyone, least of all God. Yet they do not realise that they are not free at all: they are slaves to their own lusts and desires, which will only bring forth sin and death.

"I will not go out free"

There is an interesting parallel here with Exodus 21 concerning laws about slaves. In verses 1-6 we read that a slave was to serve for six years, but in the seventh he was to be set free.

However, if the slave said, "I love my master ... I will not go out free" (verse 5), he was to be brought before God, to the door or the doorpost. His master would bore a hole in his ear and he would serve his master forever.

We too are slaves. Though once enslaved to sin, we have been set free by the blood of the Lamb. Having declared our loyalty to God before many witnesses – "I love my master ... I will not go out free" – we now present ourselves before God as slaves to righteousness, leading to sanctification and *eternal life* (Romans 6:16-22). This was foreshadowed in Exodus 21:6, where we read that the slave would serve his master *forever*, pointing forward to the resurrection and reward of the faithful.

The flesh tells us that we are free to do as we please, to serve ourselves and to give in to our own desires, but we have promised to listen only to the voice of our Master, as loyal slaves to righteousness. The Hebrew slaves had their ears bored through with an awl, surely as a symbol that they would forever listen to and obey their master. Making a hole in this way was a permanent, irreversible action. (I used to have my ears pierced and the marks are still there, fifteen years later.) In the same way, our commitment to God is permanent. Even if we turn our back on God, He will never turn His back on us because His loyalty is perfect and He will accomplish all that He has purposed. Although Israel broke their covenant with God, He told them through Ezekiel:

> "I will remember my covenant with you ... and I will establish for you an everlasting covenant ... and you shall know that I am the LORD." (16:60,62)

Open the door

There is one final point to consider in Exodus 21. It is not insignificant that the slave had to approach the door. We know that the door is a symbol taken up time and again in scripture. Jesus said, "I am the door. If anyone *enters by me*, he will be saved" (John 10:9), and again in Revelation 3:20, "Behold, I stand at the door and knock. If anyone *hears my voice* and *opens the door*, I will come in to him and eat with him, and he with me". Notice the action required on our part: we have to be listening out for the voice of the Master and we have to respond by opening the door. While the slave of Exodus 21 was brought by his master to the doorpost and before God, we have the living word of God to teach us how to recognise the voice of our Master and to guide us to the door. If we remain loyal to our Master, circumcising our hearts and walking blamelessly before him, we shall recognise the voice when Jesus comes a second time, "with a cry of command, with the voice of an archangel, and with the sound of the trumpet of God" (1 Thessalonians 4:16). Finally, God's covenant with Abraham will have its fulfilment and the whole world will know that God keeps His promises and rewards the loyalty of His chosen people.

Questions and suggestions

- Consider how loyal God is to you – how He keeps all His promises. How loyal are you to Him?
- Is loyalty to your brothers and sisters more important to you than your own needs and desires? How can you show this in the way you behave towards them?
- Are you more loyal to your job than your ecclesia? To your hobbies or to ecclesial gatherings? To your friends outside the Truth, or to your brothers and sisters?

Chapter 13
M for Meditation

"Let the words of my mouth and the meditation of my heart be acceptable in your sight, O LORD, my rock and my redeemer." (Psalm 19:14)

THE verse above paints such a beautiful picture of humble discipleship. True disciples will desire, above all else, to please God in the things that they think, do and say, for He alone is our rock and our redeemer.

What is the meditation of your heart? What are the thoughts that most often fill your mind? How much spiritual food does your mind receive when compared to the constant force-feeding it receives from the world?

It does not come naturally to us to think on the things of God. So often, the lust of the eyes, the lust of the flesh and the pride of life get in the way. We covet, desire and boast on a daily basis, often without a second thought. God declared in Genesis 6:5 that the thoughts of man's heart were "only evil continually". Centuries later, Jesus said that "out of the heart of man come evil thoughts, sexual immorality, theft, murder, adultery, coveting, wickedness, deceit, sensuality, envy, slander, pride [and] foolishness" (Mark 7:21,22). He explained that "the good person out of the good treasure of his heart produces good, and the evil person out of his evil treasure produces evil, for out of the abundance of the heart his mouth speaks" (Luke 6:45).

If the meditations or thoughts of our heart are to be pleasing and acceptable to God, we need to ensure that we are storing up the right things in our hearts in the first place. We must ask ourselves honestly: what does my heart treasure? Do I get more excited about the upcoming Fraternal or the latest film release? Do I cherish the word of God, or would I rather read a novel or magazine? Do I delight to speak with my friends and family about the scriptures, or do I prefer to talk about my achievements, goals and latest adventures? Do I spend more time making plans for this life than I do making preparations for eternal life in God's kingdom?

Be transformed

If our hearts treasure the things of the world, we shall begin to think and act like the world, but if we treasure the things of God, storing up His word in our hearts, we shall think and act more like Him. This is why we are exhorted in Romans:

> "Do not be conformed to this world, but be transformed by the renewal of your mind." (12:2)

The Greek word here translated "transformed" is *metamorphoō*, from which we have the English word 'metamorphosis'. When an insect undergoes complete metamorphosis, this is usually accompanied by a change of nutrition source or behaviour.[1]

---

1   en.wikipedia.org/wiki/Metamorphosis

This is interesting to us because we know that a spiritual metamorphosis or transformation also requires that we feed hearts with spiritual food, and that this should result in a change of behaviour as this food impacts our thoughts and actions.

We know, of course, that the spiritual food we require is the "sincere milk of the word" (1 Peter 2:2, KJV) which is "sweeter than honey" (Psalm 19:10). This is why we are to meditate on it: to ponder, consider, contemplate, muse, ruminate, think and weigh up every part of scripture and apply it to our own lives. It has a transformative effect on our hearts and minds. It draws us away from the mindset of the world and fills our treasure stores with something far greater than gold or precious jewels: the wisdom and understanding of God (see Psalm 49:3).

We can only do this effectively when we set aside quiet time in which to be still and drink in God's word of life, to ponder the way in which He is powerfully working in our lives, and to stand in silent awe as we contemplate His creative and transformative power. There is no right or wrong way to meditate on these things, but what follows are several suggestions.

Hymns

Our Christadelphian hymn book can be a helpful aid to meditation. Whatever your circumstance, however you are feeling, there will always be an appropriate hymn to express this. It might not always be appropriate to sing a hymn out loud, but reading the words slowly and thoughtfully, applying what you read to your own life and allowing the thoughts expressed to sink in, can be incredibly cathartic and bring peace to the chaos of everyday life. What's more, the next time you sing that particular hymn, it will resonate on a much more personal level than before.

Music

Listening to music can also help us to focus on the things of God. There is plenty of scripturally sound music available to us, produced by various groups and individuals within the brotherhood,[2] along with music produced by outside sources which take texts entirely from scripture.[3] Perhaps you already listen to this kind of music in the car or as background music to everyday tasks.

When we set aside time to listen to this music without distraction, however, focusing on the words, meditating on the ideas expressed and their application to our own lives, the music can impact us even more positively by filling our hearts and minds with scripture and helping to replenish our treasure store.

Choose a Psalm

The book of Psalms is like a banquet for the hungry disciple: there is so much food to choose from! Yet there is little benefit or enjoyment to be gained from hurriedly swallowing it whole. It is far better to savour each bite and to spend time chewing each mouthful.

One way in which you could use the Psalms – or indeed any suitable passage – to meditate is to read your chosen Psalm slowly, line by line, thinking about how each phrase applies to your own life. Immerse yourself in the emotions you feel as you read each verse. Ponder the context: how did it apply at the time it was written, how did it apply to Christ, and how does it apply to you? Allow the words you read to change your perspective, still your anxious thoughts and renew your hope.

---

2 www.christadelphianmusic.co.uk, www.jehoshaphatmusic.com.
3 www.seedsfamilyworship.com, www.sonsofkorah.com.

Create a chart

A very useful exercise is to write down your thoughts as you spend time meditating on the Psalms. You could create a list such as the one begun below (Psalm 27:1), splitting the psalm into short phrases and writing one word next to each phrase which sums up your emotional response. This is something the young people did at a recent Bible School I attended and it was interesting to see how different everyone's responses were. This should come as no surprise, since we all lead unique lives, each with a different set of experiences and a unique combination of personality traits.

- "The LORD is my light and my salvation" – *saved*.
- "Whom shall I fear?" – *protection*.
- "The LORD is the stronghold of my life" – *safe*.
- "Of whom shall I be afraid?" – *strength*.

A four-stage approach

One approach to meditation to which I was recently introduced and have found very helpful takes a four-stage approach. The aim is to make meditation a two-way process, entering into a dialogue with God, not merely reading the word but also listening to what God has to tell us through its pages. The process is outlined below.

1. *Reading* – Choose a short passage of scripture (just a few verses). Read it several times, considering it from different angles, focusing in on different phrases, but not assigning one particular meaning.
2. *Meditation* – Consider what the passage means to you. Can you relate to it from your own experience? What impact could this have upon your thoughts and actions?

3. *Pray* – Open up a dialogue with God. Pray about the passage you have been reading and the points you have been meditating upon. Listen to what God has to say through the words of scripture.
4. *Contemplate* – Take time to be still and to savour what you have just read and experienced. Allow it to sink in.

Meditate on a theme

The Psalmist often meditated on specific aspects of his relationship with God. This surely involved not only thinking about these things, but also praying about them, since the two go hand in hand. As we begin to think more about the things of God, so prayer will flow spontaneously from our heart as we seek God and draw near to Him. You could meditate on:

- What God has done for you (Psalm 119:27; 77:12).
- God's creative power (145:5).
- God's law and statutes, and how we shall keep them (119:15, 99; Joshua 1:8).
- God's promises and our future hope (Psalm 119:148).
- God's love (48:9).

Be creative

In recent years, colouring books have taken the shops by storm. As modern life grows increasingly hectic, we become more and more aware of the need for relaxation and down time. Colouring is seen as the perfect way to relax the mind, to focus on what is directly in front of you, and to block out the incessant chatter of our overstimulated minds.

If you find sitting still and focusing your mind an almost impossible challenge, then the thought of meditating on God's word for any length of time without your mind wandering (What's for dinner? I really ought to call the plumber. Did I pay the council tax?) might seem overwhelmingly difficult. Combining meditation with art can be very effective in helping us to focus the mind and concentrate on one thing at a time.

This could be done in numerous ways. You might like to choose a passage of scripture to read, then draw or paint a picture, expressing your thoughts and feelings about the passage. Alternatively, you could listen to a passage of scripture bring read out loud and 'draw what you hear'. This works equally well with scriptural songs.

Look around you

Many of us feel closest to God and most peaceful when surrounded by the beauty of God's creation. Go to the park, the beach or local nature reserve; sit in the garden; climb a mountain; go stargazing. Stand in awe of creation and contemplate the majesty of the One who made all things. Consider the intricacy of the human body, and how scientists are baffled as to how the 'simple' cell (which is really not simple at all) could have come into existence. Allow yourself to feel very small, but loved.

Finally ...

However we choose to meditate on God's word, we know that by doing so we are filling the treasure store of our hearts with godly wisdom and understanding, which in turn will influence our words and actions for the better. "I have stored up your word in my heart", writes the Psalmist, "that I might not sin against you" (119:11). And so, renewed in the spirit of our minds, we put off the old self and put on the new self, "created after the likeness of God in true righteousness and holiness" (Ephesians 4:23,24).

"Finally, brothers, whatever is true, whatever is honourable, whatever is just, whatever is pure, whatever is lovely, whatever is commendable, if there is any excellence, if there is anything worthy of praise, think about these things." (Philippians 4:8)

Not only that, but "practise these things, and the God of peace will be with you" (verse 9).

Questions and suggestions

- What does your heart treasure? Do you delight more in the things of the world or the things of God?
- Are you feeding your heart with spiritual food?
- How will you begin to meditate more on the word of God? Choose one of the ways described in this chapter, or find one of your own, and put it into practice.
- What are the benefits of meditating on God's word?

Chapter 14
N for Now

IN my chapter about joy, I wrote about the importance of being present in the moment; how we need to stop thinking and analysing so much, and simply to appreciate what is happening right now. There is much to be said for being still, absorbing the sights and sounds around us, experiencing joy and expressing our gratitude that we can just *be*. Studies[1] have shown that those who mostly live in the present, rather than recalling the past or imagining the future, are happier and more content with their lives than those who spend most of their time ruminating on either the past or the future. However, we cannot use the present moment solely for stillness and quietness: it is also a time for action. "Look carefully how you walk", writes Paul to the Ephesians, "not as unwise, but as wise, making the best use of the time" (5:15,16).

Although we can learn from the past and be motivated by the future, we have to learn to act *now*. Since we cannot know what tomorrow holds and we cannot change the past, we should

---

1   www.thetimeparadox.com.

focus our efforts on making the most of today, doing all to the glory of God and giving the present moment our full attention. "Whatever your hand finds to do, do it with all your might", writes the Preacher in Ecclesiastes 9:10 (NIV). The reason? There is no working, planning, knowledge or wisdom in the grave.

We know that there cannot be much time left before Christ returns. Will we use the time we have wisely, regularly replenishing the oil in our lamps to ensure they are burning brightly, or will we be found sleeping?

A little sleep ...

> "I passed by the field of a sluggard, by the vineyard of a man lacking sense, and behold, it was all overgrown with thorns; the ground was covered with nettles, and its stone wall was broken down. Then I saw and considered it; I looked and received instruction. A little sleep, a little slumber, a little folding of the hands to rest, and poverty will come upon you like a robber, and want like an armed man."
>
> (Proverbs 24:30-34)

The book of Proverbs is full of warnings against laziness and complacency. Here, we read that hard work is of much value and that we can only expect to reap a reward if we put in effort now.

> "The soul of the sluggard craves and gets nothing, while the soul of the diligent is richly supplied." (13:4)

In other words, "If you are too lazy to plough, don't expect a harvest" (20:4, CEV).

If we see that there is a need to be met, we ought to act *now*, rather than wait for tomorrow. It is always easier to put something off until tomorrow, yet it will be no easier to take action tomorrow than it would have been today. Therefore, "Do not say to your neighbour, 'Go, and come again, tomorrow I will give it' – when you have it with you" (3:28). Do not waste today or rely on tomorrow, for you do not know what tomorrow will bring.

How, then, can we make the best use of our time today and remove obstacles to growth and productivity?

Good intentions

How often do you make plans, write lists and set goals? If you're anything like me, this is an almost daily occurrence. Yet how often do we see these through? The future is just a fantasy unless we use *today* to set things in motion. We can have all the good intentions in the world, but unless we put them into action, they will amount to nothing. "In all toil there is profit, but mere talk tends only to poverty" (14:23). Making plans, being organised and setting ourselves tasks are all helpful things to do, but will only benefit us if we put in the effort to follow them through.

Ask yourself: what one thing can I do today towards x, y or z? This could be making a phone call, sending an e-mail, making an enquiry, ordering equipment or something else entirely. Now go and do it!

Procrastination

Have you done it yet? If, like many, you are a procrastinator by nature, it may well be some time before you get around to it. In the meantime, you will have found plenty of other – often useful – things to do to fill your time. A natural inclination to procrastinate does not have to be a negative trait. In fact, procrastination may actually increase productivity.[2] Just

---

2   www.businessinsider.com/use-procrastination-to-get-things-done-2014-6.

think of all the tasks that get completed while you avoid that one job you should be doing! Procrastinators will not use their time effectively if they begin work on a task too long before the deadline. They will simply work more slowly, hit mental blocks and waste time. Those at the other end of the spectrum, however, work efficiently and thoroughly well ahead of schedule and tend to complete tasks in a logical order. Whichever approach you take to completing tasks, it is important to manage your time well and to spend it doing worthwhile tasks.

Few of us can claim that we are using our resources (time, knowledge, skills, possessions, connections, money) to the full. There are likely many things you have thought about doing over the past few months which seemed like a good idea at the time, but you judged them too difficult, too huge or too time-consuming. Maybe you instead sought out a task which would produce instant results, or for which you would receive recognition and praise. Perhaps the idea seemed doomed to fail, so you didn't even attempt it. Maybe you told yourself, 'I'll look into it later', but later never came. More than likely, you did nothing at all. After all, the easiest thing for us to do is that which we are currently doing (which is usually nothing).

So what are you putting off? In terms of ecclesial life, this might be:

- Organising an event;
- Joining a committee;
- Offering help;
- Attending an event;
- Visiting someone;
- Removing temptation to sin;
- Renewing good habits.

If there is something you could be doing, and there is no valid reason why you are not doing it, then there is no better time to begin than *now*. "If you wait for perfect conditions, you will never get anything done" (Ecclesiastes 11:4, TLB). We must be proactive in serving God, our families and our brothers and sisters, prayerfully taking the initiative so that God can give the growth and increase the harvest.

One king, two spies

The Bible is full of examples of men and women who did not let the perceived enormity or difficulty of a task prevent them from faithfully seeing it through.

As soon as Hezekiah acceded to the throne ("in the first year of his reign, in the first month" – 2 Chronicles 29:3), he opened the doors of the temple and restored the sacrifices and offerings there. Then, understanding the spirit of the law and not wishing to wait another year until Passover, the king declared that the Passover should be kept *in the second month*. Are we as passionate about renewing our own dedication to God? When we see that our lamp has gone out and that our doors are in a state of disrepair, do we immediately and urgently take measures to restore our faith? Do we help others to do the same?

When sent to spy out the land, Joshua and Caleb returned with a good report, encouraging the people that the land was good and should be taken immediately (Numbers 13:30; 14:6-8). Their faith helped them to see beyond the giants and the strong walls, and they wanted to act *now*. Does our faith help us to see beyond the difficulties we may face, or are we easily disheartened? Do we have the courage and passion to act *now*, or are we always putting things off, waiting for the 'right' conditions, which may never materialise?

Where do I start?

Whether you are one of those people who looks down their 'to do' list for the day with a sense of overwhelming dread and dismay, or someone who is motivated and energised to know that they have a very productive day ahead of them, one thing is certain: once momentum kicks in, it will keep you moving forward. Many people – especially procrastinators – find it helpful to start the day with a small, easy task and then to complete tasks in an order that appeals to them. The important jobs will still get done, but so will many others!

It can be helpful to prioritise each task on your 'to do' list. For example, the following numbering system can be used quickly to annotate your list and thus determine which tasks should ideally be completed first in order to make the most of the time available. This will probably appeal the most to those who have a tendency to approach tasks in a more ordered way.

	Important	Not important
Urgent	1	2
Not urgent	3	4

Manage your goals

Breaking up tasks into more manageable chunks which can be implemented straight away is vital if we are to stay focused and motivated. Without short- and medium-term goals, we can easily feel paralysed because the ultimate goal appears impossibly difficult to reach.

Spend some time thinking about your own goals, remembering to make them **SMART**:

S – specific, significant, stretching;
M – measurable, meaningful, motivational;
A – attainable, acceptable, action-oriented;
R – realistic, relevant, results-oriented;
T – time-bound, tangible, trackable.

Now take a look at the graphic below. You may find it useful to create a target chart like this for yourself. In each of the inner segments, write one of your long-term goals and give it a rating of 1-10 according to how important that goal is to you. In the next segment, write the first step you will take towards each goal, along with a deadline (within one week). The next segment contains a more medium-term goal with a deadline, and the outer segment is what your goal will look like when it has been achieved, along with an ideal deadline. This proved particularly helpful to me when I was stuck in a rut, helping me to make decisions about what I would do with my life and how I could best use the resources and skills God had given me. It gave me the motivation and vision to get off the starting block and to make much better use of my time. I've never looked back!

Do all to the glory of God

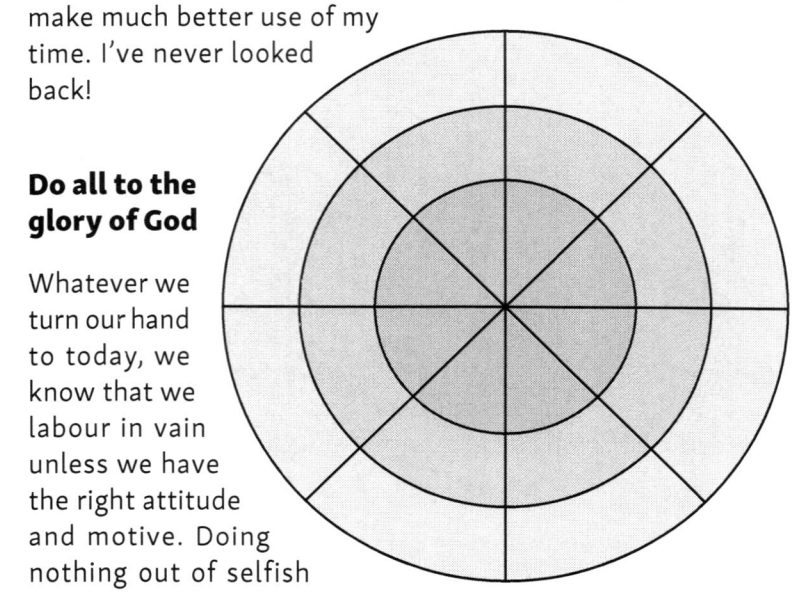

Whatever we turn our hand to today, we know that we labour in vain unless we have the right attitude and motive. Doing nothing out of selfish ambition or pride (Philippians 2:3), we should rather seek to give God the glory in everything we do, putting love at the heart of our actions. He has called us to serve Him with all our might, making the most of the time left to us, and He desires a response *today* – not tomorrow or next week.

In the words of Hymn 396, *now* is "the time to serve the Lord, to do His will, to learn His word; in death there is no power to know, far less in wisdom's way to go".

So what are you waiting for?

Questions and suggestions

- What are you putting off until tomorrow which could be done today?
- Why are you putting it off? Is your reasoning valid?
- Put down this book and go and do it!

Chapter 15
O for Optimism

THE word 'optimism' comes from the Latin word *optimum*, meaning 'the best thing'. An optimistic person will regard their past, present and future as the optimum path they could take, and will be content in any and every situation (Philippians 4:11,12). As disciples of Christ, it is important that we learn how to approach life – particularly when difficulties arise – with godly optimism.

The past

How do you view the past events of your life? Do you feel positive about the path you have trodden? Are you confident that it was the right way to go? Are you thankful for the joys and trials you have experienced? Do you view the past as a learning curve? Or do you perhaps find yourself consumed by regret? Do you sometimes doubt the road you have travelled and wish you could start all over again? Do you compare your life to that of those around you and experience feelings of inadequacy and discontentment?

Whatever may have happened in the past, it is our current attitude that matters. No good has ever come from bewailing the past, which we are utterly unable to change. Guilt, shame, resentment and regret are all natural reactions to negative situations, but they are not long-term solutions. Guilt must give way to forgiveness, shame to humility, resentment to understanding and regret to acceptance. It is possible to reframe the past, in order to approach it more optimistically. Consider:

- Is my relationship with God stronger as a result of this trial?
- What have I learnt about myself, others and God?
- Has it brought me closer to my friends, family and ecclesia?
- Am I better able to empathise with others because of my experiences?
- Am I thankful for the lessons I have learnt?
- Has it made me pray more earnestly for the kingdom?

If not, perhaps it is time for a change of perspective.

There is nothing in our past that is hidden from God, and He does not let His children suffer for no reason:

> "For the Lord disciplines the one he loves, and chastises every son whom he receives. It is for discipline that you have to endure. God is treating you as sons. For what son is there whom his father does not discipline?" (Hebrews 12:6,7)

Every trial is an opportunity for growth, but only if we are willing to listen and learn.

The Apostle Paul suffered many things: hunger, beatings, imprisonments and shipwreck; yet he learnt to view all of these trials with godly optimism, so that he was able to say:

> "We rejoice in our sufferings, knowing that suffering produces endurance, and endurance produces character,

and character produces hope, and hope does not put us to shame." (Romans 5:3-5)

If we, too, can view our past experiences and trials as stepping stones to greater empathy, a stronger faith and a firmer hope, we shall not be overcome with disappointment and regret but will come to know true peace and contentment.

The present

We considered in the last chapter how we are unable to change the past and have no control over the future, but can make the most of *now*. Whether today is filled with joy or sorrow, we can approach it with a cheerful optimism, knowing that "all things work together for good, for those who are called according to [God's] purpose" (Romans 8:28). We cannot know how the events of today will impact upon the rest of our lives, or how they will influence the lives of those around us. I'm sure we can all think of many times when we have greatly struggled, yet only later understood the value of that suffering. Intense trials and pressure prompt us to re-evaluate our lives and make often pivotal decisions. They might necessitate changes in location, job or lifestyle that we can now see were providential.

The Apostle Paul spent some years in chains, patiently enduring dire conditions and enjoying little freedom. He could have given up hope. He could have resigned himself to the fact that he was in prison, unable to help his brothers and sisters or spread the Gospel. He could have wallowed in self-pity and frustration, bitterness and indignation. What he did instead was to make the most of his confinement by studying the scriptures, encouraging the brotherhood and preaching the Gospel. Bound as he was, day and night, to Roman soldiers, he discovered that this was the perfect preaching opportunity; and, unlike John, who visited many ecclesias in person and expounded key principles for life in the Truth (2 John, verse 12; 3 John, verses 13,14), Paul had no option but to write these things down. How thankful we are that his chains made that necessary!

Similarly, we do not yet know what good will come out of the trials we are experiencing right now. Though they may at times feel unbearable, we must strive to remain optimistic, knowing that God can see the end from the beginning, even though we cannot. This requires that we faithfully trust that He knows best and is working out His purpose for us. We can begin by thanking God for every trial that comes our way. Though not easy to do, we have immediately reframed the situation in our minds. Rather than viewing it negatively, we begin to consider how God might be working in our lives and what He might be trying to teach us.

Another helpful and encouraging exercise is to spend time considering the way in which God has brought us through all of our past trials (cp. Deuteronomy 8:2). Think about how far He has brought you, and all that you have learned in the process. Though at the time it is never easy, God helps us to fight our giants so that we can confidently say:

> "He delivered us from such a deadly peril, and he will deliver us. On him we have set our hope that he will deliver us again." (2 Corinthians 1:10)

Armed with prayer, optimism and vision, we determinedly push on, no matter how much of a struggle that may be, knowing that this is the path marked out for us, and that the end of it is eternal life, if we remain faithful.

The future

Though we have such a positive vision of the future kingdom, it is often difficult to remain optimistic about the time remaining before Christ's return. Full of the unknown and the unfamiliar, the immediate future is a daunting place; so why do we spend so much time there, constantly dwelling on what might be, rather than what *is* and what we know for certain *will be*? If we truly believe that God is in control of the future and is directing our paths, why do we still so often fear what tomorrow may bring? If we put our trust in God and seek to do His will, He will guide our steps and take care of our needs. The Psalmist writes:

> "I have been young, and now am old, yet I have not seen the righteous forsaken or his children begging for bread. He is ever lending generously, and his children become a blessing." (Psalm 37:25,26)

The Apostle Paul, too, understood this truth:

> "And my God will supply every need of yours according to his riches in glory in Christ Jesus." (Philippians 4:19)

Our "every need" is not that we shall be happy all the time and enjoy a comfortable life. Although the world makes much of the 'pursuit of happiness' and the accumulation of wealth, these are not things with which we should concern ourselves. Our prerogative is to love and serve God in all circumstances, and to love others as ourselves (Luke 10:27). This involves sacrifice and humility: two character traits that are at odds with the dog-eat-dog world in which we live. We should not, therefore, expect our lives to take the easiest route, for we know that "the gate is wide and the way is easy that leads to destruction, and those who enter by it are many" (Matthew 7:13).

That is not to say we should be miserable all the time. There will be times when we find it extremely difficult to control our negative emotions, but it is never impossible. Rather than dwelling on negative thoughts and emotions, we can learn to acknowledge their presence and seek to replace them with positive thoughts and emotions. Memorising and reciting scripture can be a powerful way to combat feelings of anxiety and negativity as they arise, but we can also use phrases as simple as, "I choose to be happy, in spite of my circumstances". Though this may sound obvious, it is something I only tried recently, and it really works! Worry never got anyone anywhere, but a cheerful attitude makes even the worst trials bearable.

Knowing that these trials – big and small – *will* come, why do we spend so much time worrying that they *might*? We have already considered how God disciplines those whom He loves, and we know from scripture that He will also provide a way of escape (1 Corinthians 10:13) and will not let us fall completely (Psalm 37:24). Our attitude towards suffering is to be one of thankfulness and rejoicing, knowing that suffering produces endurance, builds our character and strengthens our hope (Romans 5:3-5). In suffering as Christ did, we learn to be more like him. An optimistic attitude towards future suffering will help us to be prepared when trials do come, and will rob that suffering of its power to hurt us. Instead, it will serve only to strengthen our faith.

What's more, we know that we shall never have to suffer alone. The Apostle Peter urges us to cast all of our fears and anxieties on God, because He cares for us (1 Peter 5:7), and to resist temptation, standing firm, knowing that "the same kinds of suffering are being experienced by your brotherhood throughout the world" (verse 9). God has put us in ecclesias so that we can support and encourage one another when trials do come. "And after you have suffered a little while", we are assured, "the God of all grace, who has called you to his eternal glory in Christ, will himself restore, confirm, strengthen, and establish you" (verse 10).

No suffering lasts forever. Even if there are trials we must endure during our mortal existence, we know that the time is coming when:

"[God] will wipe away every tear from [our] eyes, and death shall be no more, neither shall there be mourning, nor crying, nor pain any more, for the former things have passed away." (Revelation 21:4)

While many in the world today, encouraged by the scare tactics of the media, are terrified about what the future will bring, we know that we do not need to worry. As we see men's hearts failing them for fear, we can take courage, full of optimism and hope, because we know that Christ will surely return soon. Rather than being afraid, we are to "look up, and lift up [our] heads; for [our] redemption draweth nigh" (Luke 21:28, KJV). "Even so, come, Lord Jesus"!

Questions and suggestions

- Is there a past event in your life about which you still harbour negative feelings? Think about ways in which you could reframe that event. What have you learnt? Has it drawn you closer to God?
- What are you struggling with right now? Imagine yourself in five years' time, looking back. How might this current struggle have shaped your life? Did it lead to a better understanding of others' struggles? Did it strengthen your trust and dependence on God?
- Do you have a vision of the future – of the light at the end of the tunnel? Meditate on the things of the kingdom and notice how a clear sense of direction and ultimate goal enables you to feel optimistic about the past, present and future.

Chapter 16
P for Prayer

PRAYER is not simply a task to be done, a self-contained activity, it is a relationship. Unless we strive to develop and improve this aspect of discipleship our relationship with God will not grow. How is your prayer life? Do you pour out your heart before God regularly, honestly and fervently, or has prayer become something of a ritual or tradition? God invites us to have a rich and dynamic prayer life in which we not only give Him praise, but also ask Him for help and guidance in our own lives and the lives of those around us. Prayer is very personal to each of us: there are no rules or rituals to obey. All God asks of us is that we seek Him regularly, earnestly and humbly for He has promised:

> "When you seek me with all your heart, I will be found by you." (Jeremiah 29:13)

The uncomfortable truth

Developing an open and honest relationship with God can be a difficult and at first uncomfortable process. To ask for His help is to admit that we are not as strong as we might think we are, and that we are not in control of our own lives. To voice our darkest thoughts is to confess that we so often lose our battle against temptation and sin. In prayer, we come face to face with things we would rather keep locked away. We face the uncomfortable truth that we are not perfect and we need help.

Since nothing is hidden from God, we should not seek to present Him with half-truths and half-hearted excuses. Instead, we must offer Him our whole hearts and our whole minds. We admit that we are weak and vulnerable, secure in the knowledge that God will never take advantage of our weaknesses, but will use them to make us stronger. For we trust that God has chosen us *in spite* of all of these imperfections.

"My grace is sufficient for you, for my power is made perfect in weakness." (2 Corinthians 12:9)

We know this quote well, but do we ever stop to think about the next part of the same verse?

"Therefore I will boast all the more gladly of my weaknesses, so that the power of Christ may rest upon me."

We ought to *"boast"* of our weaknesses, to rejoice in them and to find them a source of confidence, knowing that God works with broken, contrite men and women to mould and shape them into His image. We can drop the strong, confident persona that we feel the world requires of us because we know that God looks deeper and asks for a much more genuine relationship with each of us.

"But this is the one to whom I will look: he who is humble and contrite in spirit and trembles at my word." (Isaiah 66:2)

The more open we are with God about our weaknesses and failings, the deeper and closer will be our relationship with

Him. In pouring out our hearts to Him in this way, we are no longer praying out of habit, but out of a desire to have a strong, trusting relationship with our Creator. We find peace, secure in the knowledge that God loves us and hears our prayers, knowing that we have Jesus as our High Priest and mediator. We find freedom because we no longer have to hide from God or ourselves, no longer need to pretend we are perfect when we quite clearly are not. We know that we are ragged and torn, but we also know that we have been clothed with righteousness and seated in heavenly places, carried and lifted up by an awesome God, for –

> "there is none like God ... who rides through the heavens to your help, through the skies in his majesty. The eternal God is your dwelling place, and underneath are the everlasting arms." (Deuteronomy 33:26,27)

Esteeming others

Whilst it is important to build a close relationship with God and to feel able to tell Him everything that is going on in our lives, we cannot neglect our responsibility to our brothers and sisters. To pray only about our own circumstances, worries and plans would be to miss the point entirely, since we are called to "esteem others better than ourselves" (Philippians 2:3). We ought rather to follow the example of our Lord Jesus who, on the night he knew he would be betrayed, when he was almost overwhelmed with sorrow and fear, lifted up his eyes and prayed for his disciples and for all those who would come to believe the Gospel message.

There are many ways in which we can ensure our prayers are appropriately balanced. Some like to use the acronym **ACTS**: Adoration, Confession, Thanksgiving, Supplication. Others take the Lord's Prayer as a structural basis for their own prayers:

thanks and praise, forgiveness, prayer for those in need, guidance and requests. One family I know has seven areas of focus for their morning prayers, one for each day of the week. These include the ecclesia, preaching work and family.

The Prayer Journal, available from the Christadelphian Office, contains several pages of suggestions regarding the possible structure and content of prayers. The Journal also provides additional suggestions for each day of the year, such as "preaching the Gospel", "strength to overcome weakness" and "family concerns" and there is space to record the content of each day's prayers. It can also be used to note down any matters of welfare that are mentioned in the Sunday announcements, so that these can be included in our prayers too.

Putting it into practice

The theory is all well and good, but in practice this depth of prayer and petitioning does not come naturally to us and requires patience and persistence. We need to accept that it will be hard at first, but that our perseverance will pay off. We are creatures of habit and most of us work best when we have a routine, so one idea would be to set aside a particular time every day to pray – out loud if possible – in an honest, open way. This prayer time could be first thing before getting out of bed, during breakfast, in the car on the way to school / college / university / work, during our lunch break ... Any time will do, as long as it is consistent. Research shows that we must do something around thirty times before it becomes a habit, meaning that after just one month this prayer time should start to come naturally. Why not try it? Set yourself a thirty-day challenge and determine to pray at least one meaningful prayer, at a set time or times, every day for a month.

At home, we can leave visual reminders for ourselves so that we are frequently reminded to refocus our minds and to pray. These reminders could be as direct as, "Don't forget to pray!" or more subtle messages and quotes. The extent to which you do this very much depends on your style, but such visual reminders could include:

- Strategically placed sticky notes.
- Postcards, canvases or pictures with inspirational quotes.
- Cutting out large, colourful letters to write out a wall-length Bible quote.
- Magnetic letters / words on the radiator, fridge or boiler.
- Collages of motivational pictures and quotes.
- Messages on mirrors, fridges, windows or whiteboards using non-permanent pen, glass chalk or old lipstick.
- Messages on bathroom tiles using bath crayons.

Two ears, one mouth

It is important always to remember that prayer, as with any other communication, is a two-way process involving both speaking and listening. One of my colleagues daily points out to the children in her class that God gave us two ears and one mouth, and we should use them proportionately! If we are not putting in the effort to listen to what God has to say to us through His word, we cut ourselves off from the primary way in which He speaks to us. God can and does answer prayers in other ways, but so often we find clear answers when we spend focused time reading the scriptures.

You may have heard the phrase, "Garbage in, garbage out!" How true this is! If we fill our minds with the mundane and the worldly, not only will our prayers be selfish and shallow, but we will not be receptive to what God desires to show us. If, on the other hand, we spend time reading and meditating upon His word, we attune ourselves to God's thinking and will find that our prayers become much more God-focused. We shall pray less selfishly, more thankfully, and with greater understanding. Not only this, but as we turn our attention to the word of God and away from the world, we shall begin to discover answers to our prayers in the most unlikely of Bible passages. This might happen as we are reading, but could equally happen at any time, when a verse we didn't even know we had memorised suddenly springs to mind to provide insight or comfort. God's word truly is living and active (Hebrews 4:12).

The privilege of prayer

When we pray, we ought always to do so with a humble heart, acknowledging that God's thoughts are far higher than our thoughts, and His ways much higher than our ways (Isaiah 55:9). We confess our faults and weaknesses, take off our masks, tear down the walls we have built up, and can truly be ourselves. We draw near to God, and He delights to draw near to us (James 4:8). What a powerful, humbling privilege this is, and one we must never take for granted.

We know that "the effectual fervent prayer of a righteous man availeth much" (James 5:16, KJV). The ESV renders this, "The prayer of a righteous person has *great power* as it is working". Never forget how powerful your prayers can be, when you pray with the right attitude. This means always praying "your will, not mine, be done", recognising that God gives us what we *need*, not what we want, and understanding that there are some trials we must endure because God, in His wisdom, knows they will help us to grow. It means accepting that the answer will not always be immediately apparent, and it might not be the answer we had expected or imagined. (It will be better!)

Sometimes, the answer will be "no" or "not yet". Always, the answer will be just what we need, at just the right time and in just the right way to help us grow as disciples of Christ as we await his return.

Questions and suggestions

- Is there anything in your life which you find difficult to take to God in prayer? What is holding you back from being completely honest with God? Make a conscious effort to pray about this every day, even if it only takes up one sentence of your prayer. It will get easier as time goes on.
- How balanced are your prayers? Do you thank and praise God as often as you petition Him? Do you pray more for others or for yourself? What will you do to restore a better balance?
- What time of day will you set aside to pray? Be realistic: does praying before bed suit you or will you always be too tired? Is lunchtime the best time, or will you get distracted by e-mails, phone calls and colleagues? Choose somewhere quiet and peaceful if you can. Some people like to have a "prayer chair", which they always sit on to pray, because the association helps them to focus.
- Are you listening to God as much as you are talking to Him? Don't expect God to listen to you if you don't listen to Him! Make sure you are setting aside time every day to read and meditate upon His word.

Chapter 17
Q for Quietness

HOW important is quietness to you? Do you bustle around, enjoying the cacophony of chaos that accompanies modern life, purposefully filling rare silence with background noise from the radio or TV? Does silence make you feel uncomfortable? Do you ever give yourself time to be alone with your thoughts, or to sit in silence and think about nothing at all? Would you feel guilty if you did?

In this chapter, we consider the benefits of quietness for our mental, physical and spiritual well-being.

The science of silence

Before technology brought music, TV and online entertainment into our homes, life was a lot quieter. Silence was normal and no one was afraid of it. Today, many people cannot bear it. They fill their lives with noise: music, YouTube videos, radio and TV programmes – anything to plug the silence. Yet quietness is important. Our brains need it. You might be tempted to think that listening to calming music is just as relaxing as enjoying complete silence, but studies have shown that this is not the case. True quietness is what will benefit us the most.

An increasing amount of research is being conducted by scientists into the benefits of silence for our mental and physical well-being. We now know that too much noise can cause high blood pressure, disrupted sleep patterns, stress and tension, and can also worsen symptoms of depression.

We too often overload our brains with background noise, making it more difficult to focus on the conversation we are having or the thoughts we are thinking. Our brains have to work far harder than they would if there was no noise to contend with and we are left mentally exhausted. We find it harder to concentrate, solve problems and come up with new ideas.

Thankfully, even just a few minutes of silence can have a wonderfully restorative effect on our frazzled brains. It gives us a chance to recharge, calm our overworked senses and focus on the present.

Houses, gardens and mountains

When we read about the Lord Jesus in the Gospels, we often read that great crowds gathered around him. It must have been difficult to find quietness and solitude when so many people wanted to talk to him, to hear him speak, and to be healed. Surrounded by so many people, so much of the time, would have been exhausting enough, but Jesus also had the added weight of knowing their thoughts and empathising with their emotions.

Knowing he would not be in a fit state to serve others if he was permanently exhausted and mentally overloaded, Jesus made time for quietness and solitude. This was surely one reason for his frequent visits to Bethany, to the house of Martha, Mary and Lazarus. These visits would have been a welcome and necessary retreat for both Jesus and his disciples: time spent away from the noise and the crowds; time to enjoy good company and the peace and quiet of village life.

We, too, know how refreshing it is to spend a weekend in good company, away from the world's clamour. The busier and more stressful life is, the more important it is to make time for friends and family, not only for our own well-being, but also to maintain these valuable relationships. If we find we are so busy that we never seem to spend time with those we love, then we are too busy and something needs to change.

Quiet time surrounded by the beauty of creation – be it in the garden or up a mountain – brings calm and balance into our lives. Reacting to Job's utter distress, Elihu told him to "stop and consider the wondrous works of God" (Job 37:14). Focusing on God's creation not only helps to calm our racing minds, but also puts everything into perspective.

The Garden of Gethsemane was an important place for Jesus and his disciples. The night of his betrayal was not the first time they had visited this quiet, secluded garden. Close to bustle of the city, yet a world away in its peacefulness, it would have been the perfect place to go when they needed to get away from the crowds and the noise.

Sometimes Jesus needed to be alone, away from even his closest disciples, and so we read in Matthew 14 that –

> "... after he had dismissed the crowds, he went up on the mountain by himself to pray. When evening came, he was there alone." (verse 23)

This time spent in prayer was part of what kept him going. It gave him the strength to face another day, to keep obeying the word of his Father, and to focus on the joy that lay before him. Not only this, but it gave him time and space quietly to cast the burdens of the day on the Almighty God, who neither slumbers nor sleeps.

There is a definite connection here between quietness and solitude, and prayer. Do we see prayer only as a means of communicating with our Heavenly Father? Or do we also see it as time out from the bustle of the world – time to refocus, to sit in silence, and to still our anxious thoughts? Have you ever considered that perhaps prayer is crucial for our physical and mental well-being as well as our spiritual well-being? Might this change the way in which you view prayer?

Solitude is not selfish

In retreating from the crowds, Jesus was ensuring he was physically and emotionally strong enough to minister to others and to live a life of obedience to his Father. We all know from experience that we resist temptation far better when we are calm and well rested. For Jesus, resisting temptation was crucial if he was to fulfil his purpose as the great High Priest.

Although we know we shall never live up to the standard the Lord Jesus has set us for our lives, there is certainly wisdom in following his example and ensuring we take time out when we need to. When our minds are rested, we are more patient, gentle and kind. We do not lose our temper so easily, and we are more prepared to fight temptation.

We should not feel guilty about taking time out – be it ten minutes to sit in the garden and pray, or a day out in the countryside – because we know that solitude is a God-given mechanism to help us process thoughts and emotions. This is particularly important if we are feeling overwhelmed with the challenges of life. Jeremiah understood this when he wrote:

"The LORD is good to those who wait for him, to the soul who seeks him. It is good that one should wait quietly for the salvation of the LORD. It is good for a man that he bear the yoke in his youth. Let him sit alone in silence when it is laid on him." (Lamentations 3:25-28)

Times of solitude and quiet prayer allow us to process thoughts and emotions, and to move forward with a healthier perspective.

He restores my soul

Quietness is essential for our mental, physical and spiritual well-being. God did not speak to Elijah upon Mount Horeb through the earthquake, wind or fire but with a still, small voice. How are we to hear this quiet whisper if we are always rushing around, surrounded by constant noise, and bombarded by the incessant chatter of our own minds? It is so important to take time out to be alone with God, whether in silent prayer, meditation on His word, or a quiet state of awareness.

Consider the words of Psalm 23:

"The LORD is my shepherd; I shall not want. He makes me lie down in green pastures. He leads me beside still waters. He restores my soul. He leads me in paths of righteousness for his name's sake." (verses 1-3)

Here, the Psalmist paints a picture of the quietness, stillness and calm that can be ours when we rest in the Lord and wait patiently for Him (Psalm 37:7). God is our shepherd and will make sure that we are safe and well provided for. He is in control. He doesn't make us wander alone through a barren, parched wilderness, looking for green pastures, fresh water and a safe place to rest; He lovingly leads us there and invites us to stay with Him.

There is no place here for striving and stress. This is the place to which we come when the tempest winds are battering our sails, our bodies are weary and our minds are overcome with the cares of this life. We come to rest and graze in God's pastures and to drink from the well of living water that never runs dry. Shutting the door on the noise and chaos of the world for a while, we spend quiet time alone with God so that, restored and renewed, we are ready to face the trials of life with fresh determination and strength.

Aspire to live quietly

So far, we have considered quietness and solitude as discrete moments: time taken away from the bustle of everyday life. Yet quietness is also a way of life and a desirable characteristic for the disciple of Christ.

In the world, success is measured by how busy we are, how much responsibility we have at work, how much we earn, how high-flying our children are, how big our house is, and how many expensive possessions we own. The more tired and overworked we are, the more impressed people seem to be. To live up to these standards usually requires that we work extremely long hours, neglect our families, ignore signs of mental and physical exhaustion, and bring up our children to do the same.

Is this the kind of life to which we have been called? How does God measure success?

> "Better is a handful of quietness than two hands full of toil and a striving after the wind."

The Preacher wrote this in Ecclesiastes 4:6. In this short book, we read time and again of the pointless vanity of pursuing wealth and status. It will not bring us happiness. We need to find a better balance – working to live, not living to work.

On no account should we use this as an excuse to be lazy, for "sweet is the sleep of the labourer" (5:12). We ought instead to work quietly, to earn our own living and to avoid idleness (2 Thessalonians 3:11,12), obeying our earthly masters with sincerity, and "work[ing] heartily, as for the Lord and not for men" (Colossians 3:23). In the words of the Apostle Paul, we should "aspire to live quietly" (1 Thessalonians 4:11).

This applies not only to those who go out to work, but also to those who work at home. Housework, childcare and looking out for the welfare of our brothers and sisters are all ways in which we labour, but if we overburden ourselves, we run the risk of burning out. Part of the problem is that our inner critic is constantly telling us that we are not doing enough, that we are wasting time if we are not busy, and that we should be keeping up with the Joneses (house spotless, lawn manicured, windows gleaming, children seen and not heard). We pile immense pressure on ourselves, and to what end?

> "What gain has the worker from his toil? ... I perceived that there is nothing better for them than to be joyful and to do good as long as they live; also that everyone should eat and drink and take pleasure in all his toil – this is God's gift to man." (Ecclesiastes 3:9,12,13)

If we are so close to burning out that we no longer take pleasure in life, are too irritable to show kindness to others, and have no time or energy to enjoy the fruits of our labour, then we will never appreciate God's gift to man. Life will be miserable.

It is okay to earn less and have more time for family and ecclesia. It is okay to live in a small house or flat. It is okay to say 'no' to commitments that would gain the praise and acclamation of peers but bring unnecessary stress into your life. It is okay to have a dusty mantelpiece and a messy playroom.

It is okay if there are weeds in the garden and spatters of mud on the car. It is okay to sit down and do nothing once in a while.

Aspire to live quietly, to make more time for God, family, friends and ecclesia. Cut out unnecessary stress and toil, stop pursuing wealth and the praise of men, stop comparing yourself to the Joneses (who, by the way, are a figment of your imagination) and start enjoying the gifts God has given you.

As we make space for quietness in our lives and aspire to live quietly, not rushing around and pursuing acclamation and promotion, but rather being "content to fill a little space, if [God] be glorified" (Hymn 137), we shall begin to notice the positive impact of this quietness and calmness on our character. We shall deal better with negative emotions, feel more motivated and focused, remain calm under temptation and pressure, and discover we have time to appreciate the joys and blessings of life. We shall learn to be still, to wait patiently for God, and to listen for that still, small voice of calm that leads us beside still waters and restores our souls.

Questions and suggestions

- Do you ever find yourself filling silence with unnecessary background noise? Challenge yourself to go a day – or even a week – without background noise. Turn off the car radio, put your phone on silent, use technology purposefully and mindfully, and reap the benefits of a calmer, more focused mind.
- How do you spend your evenings and weekends? Are they as busy and stressful as a working day? Do they need to be? What could you cut out in order to have more quiet time, either alone or with others?

- Are there any unnecessary events or commitments you could cut out of the next few months and replace either with a quiet weekend at home, or with a visit to / from friends / family?
- What changes could you make in your life in order to find a few moments of quiet and calm each day? You could try going for a walk during your lunch break. After work / school, try ditching screen time (temporarily or permanently) in favour of quiet activities, many of which now seem so old-fashioned to us yet are wonderfully relaxing: knitting, sewing, drawing, painting, woodwork, model making, reading, writing, baking, gardening or playing board games.

Chapter 18
R for Reliance

THINK about the people in your life whom you consider the most reliable. If they say they will be somewhere, you can be confident that they will be there. If they say they will do something, you know that they will do it, and do it well. They are loyal, trustworthy and dependable. You know this, because they have proved time and again that this is the case. They never let you down.

The faithful God

These are all characteristics which the Lord God fulfils completely. He is more reliable than anyone you or I have ever met. He is always there when we call on Him, day or night, for He does not slumber or sleep. He always keeps His promises – and how great are these promises, both for our life now and for the future! God has promised to establish Jesus as King over all the earth, and He has promised immortality and everlasting peace for those who love Him. While we wait for that day, God has promised that He will never leave or forsake us. To those who know His name and hold fast to Him in love, He has promised:

> "When he calls to me, I will answer him; I will be with him in trouble; I will rescue him and honour him. With long life I will satisfy him and show him my salvation." (Psalm 91:15,16)

We have faith that what God has spoken, He will do. This is not blind faith, for we know God's character. From our reading of scripture, from history and from our own experience, we know that God is consistent and unchanging, and that He always keeps His word. We can rely on Him for, "He who calls [us] is faithful; he will surely do it" (1 Thessalonians 5:24).

Moses understood this:

> "Know therefore that the LORD your God is God, the faithful God who keeps covenant and steadfast love with those who love him and keep his commandments, to a thousand generations." (Deuteronomy 7:9)

Can you imagine a thousand generations? Moses is clearly making the point here that God will never break His covenant with those who love Him.

Solomon was living proof that God could be relied upon to keep His word. He prayed:

> "O LORD, God of Israel, there is no God like you, in heaven above or on earth beneath, keeping covenant and showing steadfast love to your servants who walk before you with all their heart; who have kept with your servant David my father what you declared to him. You spoke with your mouth, and with your hand have fulfilled it this day." (1 Kings 8:23,24)

God had promised David that his son would sit on the throne. True to His promise, God set up Solomon's kingdom and made him prosper.

Since God's track record for keeping His promises is perfect, we can be confident that He will also keep those promises yet to be fulfilled. If God fulfilled His promise to David in the short-term by establishing Solomon's reign, He will surely establish the kingdom of the greater Son of David, the Lord Jesus Christ.

"I have spoken"

"You spoke with your mouth, and with your hand have fulfilled it this day", we read above. Solomon is making a connection here between God's word and His actions – a theme which is widespread in the book of Ezekiel, where God uses His own covenant name as a token of assurance that the things He has said will really come to pass:

> "I am the LORD; I will speak the word that I will speak, and it will be performed." (Ezekiel 12:25)

> "I am the LORD. I have spoken; it shall come to pass; I will do it." (24:14)

If we truly know and trust God, we too should need no further assurance than this!

History has seen the fulfilment of so many prophecies – many in our own lifetimes – and this strengthens our conviction that God's word is reliable, and that He keeps His promises. Yet all of this can seem so distant to us. Like David, Solomon and Ezekiel, we must seek personally to know God and to understand and experience His faithfulness, in order to reach a point where we know we can rely on God because He is God, and trust that God will perform all that He has said He will because He has spoken it. The more we choose to rely on Him, the more reliable He will show Himself to be, and our trust in Him will grow and grow. Conversely, if we choose to place our trust in other things and other people, we are denying ourselves opportunities to experience just how reliable our God is.

"Some trust in chariots"

So how much do you and I really rely on God? Those living in the developed world are at an instant disadvantage in this regard. Few of us are so poor that we consciously rely on God for food, shelter and clothing. Most of us give no thought to where our next meal will come from, whether or not we shall have warm enough clothes for the winter, or where we shall sleep tonight. Those who have lived on the streets or visited third world countries, will certainly comprehend just how amazingly blessed are those in the developed world.

A bigger challenge to our faith is emotional reliance. If we believe, as I am sure we all do, that God is reliable, why do we so often live as if this were not the case? How many times in the past month have you turned to friends or family for help before turning to God in prayer? How often have you relied on worldly crutches (comfort eating, drinking, seeking the praise of men, money, shopping, addictions of any kind) for contentment, fulfilment or escapism, rather than relying on God? We know that we are to trust in the Lord with all our hearts, not relying on our own wisdom and understanding (Proverbs 3:5). We may even think that we do this quite well. Yet often, we fail to realise just how reliant we are on people and things other than God.

Ask yourself these questions:

- When I am sad, what makes me feel better?
- When I am stressed, how do I alleviate that stress?
- When I am overwhelmed or tired, what gives me a boost?
- When I am anxious, how do I take my mind off things?
- When I am afraid, who do I turn to for help?

If the answer to any of these does not involve God, then we know we are relying on something(s) more than we are relying on Him. The Bible tells us that this will not end well:

> "Some trust in chariots and some in horses, but we trust in the name of the LORD our God. They collapse and fall, but we rise and stand upright." (Psalm 20:7,8)

Perhaps you feel like you are ready to collapse and fall; like the burden of tasks, responsibilities and trials is dragging you down and nothing you do seems to make a difference. This is because we are not meant to do these things by our own strength. Remember that "the LORD upholds all who are falling and raises up all who are bowed down" (145:14). It is God who does this. There is nothing you can do to help yourself.

"Why do you weep?"

Let us take just one of the questions asked above, and consider God's solution.

'When I am sad, what makes me feel better?'

Do you phone a friend? Go for a run? Watch comedy TV? Eat far too much chocolate? Drown your sorrows? Wallow in self-pity? Or do you turn to God for comfort?

In the first book of Samuel, we are given an insight into the terrible pain and sadness of a faithful woman who wanted so much to be a mother, but who had been granted no children. "Hannah, why do you weep?" asked her husband, "And why do you not eat? And why is your heart sad? Am I not more to you than ten sons?" (1 Samuel 1:8).

Perhaps you too know how it feels to be so sad that you cannot eat or sleep; to be so overcome with sorrow that even the simplest daily tasks take an extraordinary amount of effort to complete. The Psalmist understood this kind of emotional pain:

> "Why are you cast down, O my soul, and why are you in turmoil within me?" (Psalm 42:11)

> "In the night my hand is stretched out without wearying; my soul refuses to be comforted." (77:2)

> "My heart is struck down like grass and has withered; I forget to eat my bread." (102:4)

Yet along with the problem, we are also given the solution:

> "In the day of my trouble I seek the Lord." (77:2)

> "Hope in God; for I shall again praise him, my salvation and my God." (42:11)

David and the other Psalmists knew that God was their firm foundation, relying on Him for support and refuge, because He has always shown Himself to be dependable. And God does not change:

> "But you are the same, and your years have no end. The children of your servants shall dwell secure; their offspring shall be established before you." (102:27,28)

The writer here expresses faith in a future full of blessings (security, posterity), demonstrating godly optimism and a true understanding of God's goodness, in spite of his obvious distress. Like the Psalmists, we are to look beyond our present circumstances, trusting that our sadness and trials will not go on forever, but that we "shall again praise him" (42:11) for His goodness towards us.

Let us return to Hannah. What was her solution? With a heavy heart, yet full of hope, she went up to the house of the Lord to pour out her soul before Him (1 Samuel 1:15) and God granted her request. "Go in peace", were Eli's comforting words (verse 17). Then Hannah returned to the place where she was staying and found that she was able to eat, and that her face was no longer sad. What a transformation this must have been from the weeping Hannah of verse 8, unable to eat, to a peaceful Hannah, confident that God had heard her. Such is the power of faithful prayer, borne out of a deep reliance on God.

A burden lifted

Worldly coping mechanisms will not and cannot solve our problems. In fact, they will probably make them worse, providing only temporary distraction. Yes, it is uncomfortable to feel anxious or sad, and it is stressful to feel stressed! Yet how can we lay our burden before God unless we are ready and willing to stop running away from a situation or emotion, and to accept that it is a burden? And how shall we ever know the relief of a burden lifted if we have never allowed ourselves fully to appreciate its weight, and have never taken the time to pray about it?

Our burdens – whatever they may be – help us to mature as disciples of Christ and as children of God. In trying to escape them on our own terms, or ignoring them completely, we are shunning the discipline of our Heavenly Father and unwittingly stunting our spiritual development. Rather than avoiding negative emotions and situations or relying on worldly crutches to get by, we ought instead to face problems head-on and ask for God's help, believing that He will help us because He is God, and because He has promised He will. He is reliable, faithful, dependable; He always keeps His word.

If we approach God honestly, pouring out our hearts before Him and laying our burdens at His feet, we can experience the immense relief of a burden lifted and find the strength to fight any battle that might come our way. God assures us that, if we put our trust in Him, He will give us strength to overcome. "For by you", writes the Psalmist, "I can run against a troop, and by my God I can leap over a wall" (Psalm 18:29). Trust Him; rely on Him. For with God, nothing is impossible.

Questions and suggestions

- Do you rely on God more than you rely on friends and family?
- Who do you turn to first in a crisis?
- How has God shown Himself to be reliable in your life? Has He ever let you down?
- How can you be a reliable presence in the lives of your family / friends / ecclesial family?
- What crutches do you rely on right now that stop you relying on God in times of trial?
- Are you ready to face life's challenges and hardships head-on, trusting that God will provide for you both physically and emotionally?

Chapter 19 — S for Sacrifice

WE can understand the word 'sacrifice' on many different levels. Perhaps we think of the sacrifices and burnt offerings required under the Law of Moses. Maybe our minds turn to the sacrifice of the Lord Jesus Christ and its significance for us.

In this chapter we shall consider sacrifice in a very practical sense. What kind of sacrifice does God require of you and me?

What are you sacrificing?

We often think about sacrifice in terms of giving something up. We might talk about sacrificing our time, energy, money, possessions, personal desires and even rights and privileges.

It is worth pausing for a moment to consider just how much we are sacrificing for God. How different is your life from the lives of those who do not know God? Would your friends and colleagues know you were a Christian, had you never told them? Are you making difficult sacrifices – choosing ecclesial events over social events; attending the public lecture and Bible Class over pursuing a hobby; choosing a longer commute to work over a longer commute to the meeting; turning down a once-in-a-lifetime job opportunity because the demands would leave you little time for God? Do the sacrifices you make really cause you emotional pain as you battle to make the right decision? Or do you convince yourself that spending twenty minutes reading the Bible every day and giving up two hours a week to attend the memorial meeting is sacrifice enough?

What's more, when you do choose to give things up for God, is it done begrudgingly and half-heartedly, or do you make these sacrifices cheerfully, desiring to please and obey God over satisfying your own wants and desires?

There is a stark warning for us in the book of Malachi. In the days of this prophet, the priests simply could not understand why God was displeased with their offerings. After all, they were following the rituals laid out in the law concerning burnt offerings and sacrifices. Outwardly, they seemed to be doing all the right things, but they were trying to cheat God. They offered blind, lame and sick animals, even though the law clearly stated that such sacrifices were unacceptable (Deuteronomy 17:1). Why? Because to them, this was all for show. They thought it was enough to be going through the motions. They had lost sight of why they were making these sacrifices, and why it was important to do exactly what God had asked of them. They were making up their own rules, out of convenience. They were not taking their role seriously.

Are we the same? Do we give God the dregs of our time, energy and resources? Do we serve Him half-heartedly, and only when it is convenient for us? Do we act out of feelings of obligation, rather than a genuine desire to be obedient disciples? Are we just going through the motions? Are we taking our discipleship seriously?

God wants you

If you are ever tempted to feel a little self-righteous about the few sacrifices you do make for the Truth, consider this: none of the things mentioned so far – time, energy, wealth, possessions and rights – were ever yours to begin with. A sacrifice is only a sacrifice if it has cost you something – and these things have cost you nothing. They are gifts from God, to be used in His service, to bring Him glory. Devoting them to the work of God is the right thing to do, but this can't be the kind of sacrifice God really desires. We can only truly give to God the things that are not already His. This is clearly illustrated in the scriptures. The list below shows many things which God considers to be true sacrifices, or which are better than sacrifice.

- To listen to and obey God's voice (1 Samuel 15:22).
- Thanksgiving (Psalm 50:5).
- One who orders his way rightly (Psalm 50:23).
- A broken spirit; a broken and contrite heart (Psalm 51:17).
- One who calls on the name of the Lord (Psalm 116:17).
- Prayer; lifting up of hands (Psalm 141:2).
- Righteousness and justice (Proverbs 21:3).
- To draw near to listen (Ecclesiastes 5:1).
- Steadfast love; the knowledge of God (Hosea 6:6).
- Love (Ephesians 5:2).
- Generosity (Philippians 4:18).
- Praise; the fruit of lips that acknowledge God's name (Hebrews 13:15).

Every one of us, whether rich or poor, old or young, male or female, is able to give these things to God, but this is something we must choose to do. God wants us to choose to obey Him, to listen to His voice, and to be like Him. He does not ask for material sacrifice. He wants you!

> "Now therefore, if you will indeed obey my voice and keep my covenant, you shall be my treasured possession among all peoples, for all the earth is mine." (Exodus 19:5)

Through Christ, these promises to the Children of Israel are ours too, but we must be prepared to devote our whole lives to God – not just the small, convenient parts. In addition, we must be prepared to give up everything we own, should God require it of us, clinging not to material possessions, but to the giver of these gifts. Like Paul, we should be able truthfully to declare:

> "I count all things but loss for the excellency of the knowledge of Christ Jesus my Lord: for whom I have suffered the loss of all things, and do count them but dung, that I may win Christ." (Philippians 3:8, KJV)

Is there anything in your life which you find yourself clinging to? Does anything absorb so much of your time and energy that you have little left for the things of God? Do you ever prioritise work or hobbies over ecclesial events? Are your loyalties divided?

If there is something which is turning your heart from serving and honouring God above all else, it has become an idol in your life. True sacrifice involves the giving of our whole selves to God, so we can see why idol worship has always been such an abomination to God. In sacrificing to foreign gods, the nation of Israel were showing a lack of trust, obedience and love for the Lord their God. They were giving their hearts to gods of wood and stone which could neither see, hear nor act. In the same way, when we show devotion and loyalty to someone or something over and above God, we too are effectively sacrificing to idols. God wants our whole hearts and our undivided loyalty. If there are things in our lives that are drawing us away from Him, we must cut these off. In the words of Hymn 170, our prayer ought always to be:

"Is there a thing beneath the sun
That strives with Thee my heart to share?
Ah, tear it thence, and reign alone,
The Lord of every motion there!"

Living sacrifices

Where does our motivation to sacrifice everything – to give up all for God, to turn from idols, and to dedicate our lives to Him – come from? The answer will be different for everyone, but one strong motivator is surely God's grace. Having inherited Adam's sinful nature, we know that we deserve to die. God would be entirely just in meting out this consequence of our sin. Yet He is not only a God of justice and truth, but also of mercy and love. Through the painful sacrifice of His only begotten Son, our Heavenly Father has set a precedent for us all to follow.

> "For God so loved the world, that he gave his only begotten Son, that whosoever believeth in him should not perish, but have everlasting life. For God sent not his Son into the world to condemn the world; but that the world through him might be saved." (John 3:16,17, KJV)

God gave the life of His own Son to bring you life. Nothing you or I can sacrifice for God could ever compare to that. What, then, is our response?

> "I appeal to you therefore, brothers, by the mercies of God, to present your bodies as a living sacrifice, holy and acceptable to God, which is your spiritual worship."
> (Romans 12:1)

This is the complete devotion which we have considered. An offering up of our whole lives to God. This is the most we can do, and still it does not compare to what God has done for us. The passage continues:

"Do not be conformed to this world, but be transformed by the renewal of your mind, that by testing you may discern what is the will of God, what is good and acceptable and perfect." (verse 2)

By regularly reading and meditating upon His word, talking about it with each other and studying it together, we are to align our thinking with God's. "I delight to do your will, O my God; your law is within my heart" (Psalm 40:8), must be our heartfelt cry. This was the attitude that drove Christ's every action, and it should be our driving force too.

Take up your cross

Jesus said, "If anyone would come after me, let him deny himself and take up his cross and follow me" (Matthew 16:24). He made it clear that the life of a disciple would not be easy, nor would it be without sacrifice. It does not come naturally to us to obey God and to deny ourselves. It is far easier to think and act like Adam than it is to think and act like Christ. Nevertheless, God asks for obedient, willing hearts and minds. He asks us to draw near to listen, and to respond; to seek to know Him, to be like Him, and to choose to obey His voice. He wants living sacrifices: men and women willing to devote their whole lives to Him. He wants me, and He wants you.

Are you ready to take up your cross and live the life to which you have been called?

Questions and suggestions

- What sacrifices are you making in your life in order to make more time for God and your ecclesia?

- Is there anything in your life which you cling to but know you should let go of, if you are to give your whole heart to God?
- How do you feel about the sacrifices you make? Are you pleased to serve, even when it is inconvenient, or do you feel resentment or reluctant resignation?
- Now look at the table of true sacrifices – the things you can give to God which He has not first given to you. How might you begin to implement these into your life in a meaningful way? Choose one element to work on particularly this week.

Chapter 20

T for Thankfulness

FROM an early age, children are taught to say "thank you". It is one of the basic rules of good manners and you would expect that, by the time we reach adulthood, we should be experts in thankfulness. Yet how easy it can be to plough through the day without a single thankful word or thought directed towards our Heavenly Father. God doesn't need our thanks, but we need to give it. An attitude of thankfulness towards our Father demonstrates our appreciation of His great love for us, gives us a broader, less introspective perspective on our life as disciples, and helps us to see trials as spiritual stepping stones rather than blockades. It also makes our lives – and the lives of those around us – so much more pleasant! Thankfulness breeds positivity and contentment, and these characteristics are extremely infectious.

Give thanks always

"Give thanks to the LORD, for he is good, for his steadfast love endures forever." (Psalm 136:1)

> "I will give thanks to the LORD with my whole heart; I will recount all of your wonderful deeds." (9:1)

Verses like these from the book of Psalms set a precedent for our own prayers and praises. Our priority must always be to thank God, acknowledging that all things come from Him, and that without Him we can do nothing. Being constantly mindful of this is hard when the world around us persistently tells us to look inside ourselves, to trust in our inner strength, to take pride in our personal achievements, to look after 'number one'. This is why it is crucial that we immerse ourselves daily in the word of God. The scriptures keep us grounded. They tell us to fix our eyes on God: to trust in His strength, to thank Him for the ways He is working in our lives, and to put Him first.

Ever mindful that all things come from Him, we are to "[give] thanks always and for everything to God the Father in the name of our Lord Jesus Christ" (Ephesians 5:20). If ever we become unthankful and complacent, trusting in our own strength more than in God's, we should not be surprised if He steps in to discipline us. We know that He does this because He loves us. One by one, He will remove the things that are separating us from Himself – our worldly crutches. This may happen slowly or – as in the case of Job – almost simultaneously, and since we are beset with human nature, always tempted to put ourselves first and to let pride get in the way, we know that discipline through suffering is an inevitable yet important aspect of our discipleship.

Reframing trials

When things are going well and we are feeling happy and buoyed up, it is easy to feel thankful. But what happens when life gets tough and we experience God's discipline first-hand? How easy is it to maintain a thankful attitude when troubles arise at work, when we suffer ill-health, or when our relationships become strained? When feelings of disappointment, stress, anxiety, bitterness or resentment threaten to overwhelm us, expressing thankfulness is rarely high on our list of priorities and we find that our positivity is quickly taken captive by negative, pessimistic thoughts. Yet James tells us to "count it all joy ... when you meet trials of various kinds" (1:2). Joy? Surely joy is the last thing we feel when we are under immense stress and pressure. Nevertheless, we are exhorted to reframe our present situation and to view it through God's eyes: to see the bigger picture.

> "We rejoice in our sufferings, knowing that suffering produces endurance, and endurance produces character, and character produces hope, and hope does not put us to shame." (Romans 5:3-5)

God uses our trials to teach us vital lessons and to mould our character. He does this "for our good, that we may share his holiness" (Hebrews 12:10). We can be thankful that He does, for without this discipline, we would be poor disciples: selfish, weak, ungrateful and unholy.

Thankfulness during times of trial does not come naturally, but it is a frame of mind we can certainly develop over time. We can start by setting aside time every day to focus on all the things for which we are thankful. This might be a time of quiet reflection and prayer, or we may choose to keep a 'gratitude diary' or 'thankfulness journal'. At first, we shall find it easiest to express thankfulness for the happiest, biggest blessings in life, but will soon discover that it is the small things that bring us more lasting pleasure.

Given time, this thankful mindset will become second nature and we shall find ourselves thanking God for all things – including any trials we may face. Reframing trials in the light of what we know of God's love and purpose, we shall be thankful for lessons learnt, for opportunities to develop the godly characteristics of patience, endurance, trust and hope, and thankful that we have a Father in heaven who loves us enough to discipline us. And so, day by day, we shall learn to "give thanks in all circumstances; for this is the will of God in Christ Jesus for [us]" (1 Thessalonians 5:18).

Songs of thanks

We have considered reflection, prayer and journalling as quiet ways of expressing thankfulness, but are these the only ways? The scriptures also place a lot of emphasis on the use of music and song in thanking God (e.g., Psalm 28:7). Nehemiah appointed two large choirs to give thanks when the rebuilding of the wall of Jerusalem was complete (Nehemiah 12:31). In verse 27, we read that the Levites came to Jerusalem to celebrate the dedication of the wall "with gladness, with thanksgivings and with singing, with cymbals, harps and lyres".

We should not underestimate the role which music can play in our thanks and praise to our Heavenly Father. It is important also to understand that different cultures and generations will use music in different ways, for the same purpose of thanking and praising God. However we choose to do this, we ought always to ensure that the words we sing and listen to are scripturally balanced and doctrinally sound. We also need to respect each other's feelings about worship music and work out ways of accommodating differing approaches when expressing thanks and praise. Whilst we know that God seeks an attitude of thankfulness, exactly how we express that is down to us as individuals and collectively as ecclesias.

Appreciating others

One key benefit of a thankful attitude is that we begin to be more appreciative of what we have. This is a crucial antidote to materialism, consumerism and the lust of the flesh. It can also have a huge impact upon our relationships with one another. It is so easy to take our friends and family (inside and outside the ecclesia) for granted. How might our attitude towards them change if we were to thank God for them every day? I suspect we would begin to love them more deeply, see them through God's eyes, and treat them with improved kindness and respect. We would soon begin to notice and appreciate the many unique ways in which each one of them enhances our lives.

The Apostle Paul is a good role model here, as he continually made mention of his brothers and sisters in his prayers and was always eager to tell them that he was thankful for their love and good works. He wrote:

> "I do not cease to give thanks for you, remembering you in my prayers." (Ephesians 1:16)

And again:

> "We ought always to give thanks to God for you … because your faith is growing abundantly, and the love of every one of you for one another is increasing." (2 Thessalonians 1:3)

Once we are in the habit of thanking God for the people around us, perhaps we shall find it easier to tell them just how much they mean to us, and about the positive impact they have on our lives. To hear someone tell you that they are thankful for what you do, for who you are, and for the way in which God is working through you, is such a boost. It can fix frayed friendships, strengthen family ties, and rekindle the flame of a faltering faith.

Everyday thankfulness

Such a change in thinking will inevitably affect not only the way in which we interact with others, but also the way in which we go about daily life. A positive, thankful person who is mindful of the small blessings in life and has learnt to view trials as opportunities for growth – this is the kind of person who goes through life with a spring in his step and a smile on his face. He will not let small hiccups ruin his day. Train delayed? Then it is the perfect opportunity to go for a quick walk, do the readings, or befriend that elderly man sitting alone. While others might grumble, the thankful disciple smiles and finds an optimistic way in which to reframe the current situation for the better.

Even when bigger trials come to test her faith, the disciple who has learnt to thank God in all circumstances will not let these things get the better of her. She will remember that God has promised blessings now, yes, but also sufferings. And she will see the bigger picture. With her eyes fixed firmly on the finish line, where her Master waits with arms open wide, she will run the race with determination and endurance. With so much to be thankful for, there is little room left in her head to worry about present trials. She sees them as learning curves and stepping stones, not as insurmountable brick walls. Though there will be days when she finds it hard to remain optimistic, God will always find ways to nudge her thinking in the right direction.

As for you, soon, others will pick up on this unusually positive attitude. 'Why are you so happy all the time?' they will ask. So you tell them about God's inexpressible gift of grace. You tell them that you have every reason to be thankful, for your Father in heaven "has qualified you to share in the inheritance of the saints in light" (Colossians 1:12). You tell them that you believe all things are working together for your good – whether joys or trials. You echo the words of the Psalmist, who sang:

> "I give thanks to you, O Lord my God, with my whole heart, and I will glorify your name for ever."   (Psalm 86:12)

And you mean every word!

Questions and suggestions

- Do you stand out as a positive person with a grateful attitude? If not, why not? What is holding you back? How might you begin to incorporate thankfulness into your life?
- Do you take time to thank God for all the many blessings in your life – including the trials which you know are helping you to grow?
- How do you feel most able to express your thankfulness to God?
- Does an attitude of thankfulness pervade the conversations you have with others or do you wallow in self-pity when things are going wrong, or constantly put yourself or others down? Make a conscious effort to reframe conversations in light of the wonderful things God is doing in your life, and express your thankfulness to others as well as to God. It is an infectious attitude that will boost others too.
- Do you tell others just how thankful you are that they are in your life?

Chapter 21
U for Unique

THE human body is an amazing piece of workmanship and we truly are fearfully and wonderfully made. No two people are alike. No one else looks exactly like you, or thinks and reasons the way you do. No one else possesses the same combination of skills and attributes as you. We are, each one of us, unique; yet God has called us to be one body and of one mind.

Conflicting personalities

Being so different from each other certainly has its challenges. Since we all think and act differently, it can be difficult to put ourselves in another person's shoes. Conflict and misunderstandings arise when we take our own opinions, reasoning and emotions – often influenced more by our own experiences than by the word of God – and assume that everyone else thinks in a similar way. We attempt to force everyone into the same mould but, the fact is, this simply does not work.

It can be easy to fall into the trap of thinking, "This thought or action seems logical and reasonable to me, therefore anyone who thinks or acts differently must be wrong". We ought however to acknowledge that there is almost always more than one valid action or reaction. Rather than feeling superior, the humble disciple will "do nothing from selfish ambition or conceit, but in humility count others more significant than [themselves]" (Philippians 2:3). This requires that we regard the thoughts, feelings and actions of our brothers and sisters – provided they are not unscriptural – as more important than our own, seeking to understand different points of view and to work with each other, not against each other.

Once we stop trying to force our children, parents, brothers, sisters and friends into our own imperfect mould, we can turn our focus on the Lord Jesus, whose example alone is the one which we ought to follow. The more we mould ourselves to him – and help others to do the same – the more united we shall be in our thoughts and actions. "Let this mind be in you, which was also in Christ Jesus", wrote Paul (verse 5, KJV). Doing so, we shall still be infinitely diverse, but our purpose and focus will be the same: to love and humbly serve the Lord God and our brothers and sisters. If we are all running in this same direction, it will be far more difficult to trip each other up.

The parable of the talents

We all possess different talents, given to us by our Creator, and we have a responsibility to make the most of them. They may be particular character traits (friendliness, approachability, empathy, humour, patience) or skills (teaching, speaking, baking, writing, playing the organ, organising people or events). If we are given opportunities to use or develop our skills, we must not let pride or insecurities get in the way. Jesus' parable of the talents in Matthew 25 warns us that to bury our talents is not an option for the disciple of Christ, since they are to be used in God's service. We serve Him by serving others, for "as you did it to one of the least of these my brothers, you did it to me" (Matthew 25:40).

At certain times in our lives, we must surely all have felt disheartened about our own seemingly meagre talents or flawed character. Comparing ourselves to others, we begin to question what we can give to God, how we can contribute to ecclesial life, or what difference we can make.

Maybe we listen to an enthusiastic and inspirational brother give an exhortation and feel like our own efforts are nothing in comparison. Perhaps, as older members of the ecclesia, we envy the younger brothers and sisters who are actively organising ecclesial events and inviting hordes of people back to their houses for lunch. As young people, we might feel overlooked and undervalued as members of the ecclesia. As parents of young children, we may find our hands so tied with looking after the children on a Sunday morning that we aren't able to engage in meaningful conversation with our brothers and sisters, or to concentrate on the exhortation.

Yet we must remember that we have all been given specific talents for specific reasons. We each have a different role to fulfil, with the ultimate goal of bringing God glory. He has been moulding and shaping your character and your faith since the day you were born, preparing you to respond to the challenges of ecclesial life in a way only you can; to provide the right kind of help to those who seek it; to offer a word in season; and to fulfil any ecclesial roles and duties you may undertake. You can offer something different and unique and God sees value in the things you do and say.

Wasting time wishing we were more like Brother X or Sister Y will only compound our feelings of inadequacy and discontentment, and will cause us to scorn or neglect our own God-given talents. We ought therefore to focus on what we can do, not on what we cannot. We each have to serve God in the best way we can, not burying our talents in the ground, but using the unique resources we have been given. He has prepared – and is preparing – you for a life of service, but a proactive, positive response is down to you.

God is our strength

If you have ever wondered why God would possibly choose you to do His work when there are so many others who you believe would do a much better job, then you are not alone. You are not the first to ask, "Why me?" and you certainly won't be the last.

Overwhelmed with the magnitude of the task which God was consigning him, Moses responded to God's commission with questioning, doubt and self-criticism. "Oh my Lord, please send someone else", he pleaded (Exodus 4:13), in spite of God's reassurance that He would teach Moses what he should speak (verse 12). Jeremiah, too, doubted his own ability. God called him to be a prophet to all nations, but his wary response was, "Ah, Lord GOD! Behold, I do not know how to speak, for I am only a youth" (Jeremiah 1:6). Yet both men were encouraged by the Lord God that they should not be afraid, for He would go with them, deliver them, and show them the right words to say.

When you feel overwhelmed with the burden of responsibilities and tasks, remember that God does not call you to work in your own strength, but in His:

> "For consider your calling, brothers: not many of you were wise according to worldly standards, not many were powerful, not many were of noble birth. But God chose what is foolish in the world to shame the wise; God chose what is

weak in the world to shame the strong ... so that no human being might boast in the presence of God ... as it is written, 'Let the one who boasts, boast in the Lord'."

(1 Corinthians 1:26,27,29,31)

God has chosen you to serve Him, in spite of – and perhaps even because of – your weaknesses. 'For when you feel weakest, that is when you are truly strong' (see 2 Corinthians 12:10). When you are able truthfully to say, 'I cannot do this by my own strength, but I know that with God all things are possible', this is when you truly glorify God in the things that you do.

And God does not leave us unprepared for the tasks ahead. We have considered already how He has been moulding and shaping us, preparing us to do His work and to fulfil His purpose with us. We can and must draw on the skills, characteristics and experiences He has given us – be they many or few, great or small – but we must always boast in God, acknowledging that all things come from Him and that He alone is our source of strength.

The common good

Perhaps you find yourself at the other end of the scale: confident in your abilities, aware of your talents and eager to use them. Confidence can be a great quality when used in the right way, but those who possess it must take care not to allow even a hint of arrogance or superiority to creep into the way they think or speak. We must all regularly examine our motives. Have we begun to attribute the success of our endeavours to ourselves? Are we pursuing our talents out of selfish ambition or to impress others? Are we esteeming others better than ourselves, or have we become self-absorbed? Could it be that we are so busy serving ourselves that we are neglecting to use our talents in the service of others?

In the wilderness, hungry and tired, Jesus could have used God's power for his own benefit, yet he resisted the temptation to turn stones into bread. Not long afterwards, faced with a crowd of hungry men, women and children, he used that same power to turn five loaves and two fish into a feast that fed thousands. Surely this is the pattern of humility and service we ought to follow, putting the needs of others ahead of our own and using our talents to serve them. Like the spiritual gifts in the first century, our talents should be used "for the common good" (1 Corinthians 12:7) and not for selfish gain.

One body, many members

Whether we have one, two, five or indeed a hundred talents, we must be sure to make the most of every opportunity to put them to use in God's service. But we do not serve in isolation. Just as the human body consists of many different members, so too the body of Christ (verse 20). We all have a unique role to play, but unless we work together, the body will not function in the way it ought; and if we fail to do our part, the whole body will suffer. Every member has a vital function. We must never feel like a spare part, or that we are somehow inadequate and unable to contribute, for each of us brings something special and unique to the body of Christ.

Let us therefore purpose to be generous with our talents, to use the skills and attributes we have been given, and to be eager and willing to serve one another in love. We know that God has given us exactly the tools we need in order to be able to serve Him in our own unique way, and we need not envy our brothers and sisters. We remember that we do not work in our own strength, but in God's. And, esteeming each other better than ourselves, we learn to love and appreciate our differences as we work side by side in God's service.

Questions and suggestions

- What makes you unique?
- How could you use your unique combination of skills and character traits to serve and glorify God?
- Do you ever find yourself comparing yourself to others in your ecclesia? Why is this an unhelpful attitude?
- Have you become overly confident in your talents? Might you be attributing too much success to yourself and not enough to God?
- How might you work together with others to combine your personality and skills in order to work more effectively and passionately for the common good of the body of Christ?

Chapter 22
V for Vision

IN the mind and imagination of every happy, successful, motivated person is a vision. It is a vision of hope for the future; the grand culmination of their hard labour. This vision gives them purpose, drive and a reason to get up in the morning. It gives them the motivation to push through difficulties, to remain focused when distractions abound, and to finish what they have begun.

For the disciple of Christ, a vision of where we are headed – of future glory in God's kingdom – is vital. It gives our lives meaning and it helps us to avoid temptation. When difficulties arise, those with a strong vision of what lies ahead will not lose heart, but will cling still tighter to their faith and their hope, and will not give up.

A vision of the invisible

We know well the proverb: "Where there is no vision, the people perish" (Proverbs 29:18, KJV). Though today we do not receive new revelations from God, we have sixty-six books of inspired writings to fuel our vision, give meaning and purpose to our lives, and keep us strengthened along the narrow path that leads to eternal life. Those who are ignorant of these clear visions of warning, encouragement and hope – or who choose to ignore them, pursuing rather the lust of the flesh, the lust of the eyes and the pride of life – have no hope of eternal life but will surely perish. Without vision, the "fleeting pleasures of sin" (Hebrews 11:25) would seem so much more appealing as we sought to live for today, having no sure hope for tomorrow. For this reason, it is of vital importance that we do not allow our vision to dim, but rather seek to strengthen and renew it daily.

In Hebrews 11 we read about many great men and women of faith, each with a vision which sustained them through times of trials and temptation. Moses "was looking to the reward" (verse 26) and Abraham "was looking forward to the city that has foundations, whose designer and builder is God" (verse 10). Not only did they believe that God exists; they were confident too that He would fulfil His promises and reward their faith. They looked to a time and a place that they could neither see nor fully comprehend, yet this future vision of God's kingdom on earth was powerfully real to them.

Though none of them had ever seen God, they nevertheless "endured as seeing him who is invisible" (verse 27), for, "faith is the assurance of things hoped for, the conviction of things not seen" (verse 1) and "we walk by faith, not by sight" (2 Corinthians 5:7). Our vision – and theirs too – is a vision of the invisible!

Our vision

We share the vision of these faithful men and women: the "hope of eternal life, which God, who never lies, promised before the ages began" (Titus 1:2). But how real is it to us? How can we truly comprehend something about which the scriptures say – "no eye has seen, nor ear heard, nor the heart of man imagined, what God has prepared for those who love him" (1 Corinthians 2:9)?

We cannot expect ever fully to know what eternal life in God's kingdom will be like, and when God will be all in all (15:28), but the scriptures provide us with a rich store of verses and passages to strengthen our vision and get us excited about the future. The more often we immerse ourselves in God's word and meditate on its powerful message, the stronger and clearer our vision will become.

Consider these verses in Revelation, written to the seven ecclesias, which tell of the wonderful rewards for those who overcome – for those who conquer:

- Granted to eat of the tree of life, in the paradise of God (2:7).
- Not hurt by the second death (2:11).
- Given hidden manna, and a white stone bearing a new name (2:17).
- Authority over the nations; given the morning star (2:26-28).
- Clothed in white garments; name never blotted out of the book of life; Jesus will confess their name before the Father and His angels (3:5).
- Pillars in the temple of God forever; they will bear the name of God and of New Jerusalem, and the new name of Jesus Christ (3:12).
- Granted to sit with Christ on his throne (3:21).

Can you picture yourself in white garments, bearing a new name, granted to sit on the throne with Christ? Do you believe that these things will be your reward, if you remain faithful to the end? This is our hope and our vision, and we must hold it close.

> "If then you have been raised with Christ, seek the things that are above, where Christ is, seated at the right hand of God. Set your minds on things that are above, not on things that are on earth." (Colossians 3:1,2)

Although our vision is of things unseen, it is important that we try to focus our minds on what lies ahead. "Forgetting what lies behind and straining forward to what lies ahead", wrote Paul, "I press on toward the goal for the prize of the upward call of God in Christ Jesus" (Philippians 3:13,14). It is only too easy to become wrapped up in the cares of this life, distracted by today and anxious about tomorrow, but we must strain forward to what lies ahead and leave all other cares behind. Eternal life in God's kingdom must be our focus in life.

But how do we make it our focus, when so many other cares and distractions run through our minds?

Strengthening the vision

Just as the Children of Israel had to collect manna each day of their wilderness journey, so we too need daily to immerse ourselves in the word of God. Except on the Sabbath, the manna did not last a second day, but went rotten. Our minds are like this. Can you remember what the exhortation was about two Sundays ago, or what you read in the Old Testament reading last Tuesday? Can you remember the wonderful comment made by a brother at Bible Class earlier in the week? Can you still feel the peace which you felt when you meditated on the Psalms reading yesterday? If you are anything like me, the honest answer will be 'no'. It is so easy to forget what we have heard or read, and unless we regularly replenish the store of scripture running through our minds, we soon run out of fuel.

Daily Bible reading should never, therefore, be seen as a chore, but as the only sure way of replenishing the store of God's word in our hearts. The more time we spend reading it, the more we shall grow to delight in it. Sitting down to immerse ourselves in the pages of scripture will bring us a profound sense of peace and joy, and we shall be sorry when we have to stop.

Sitting down and doing the daily readings is not the only way to fill our minds with the word of God and strengthen our faith and vision. We can listen to an audio Bible, listen to talks or scripture-based songs, read one of the many books written by our brothers and sisters, or do our own Bible study. We can also endeavour to surround ourselves with like-minded people, making an effort to keep in touch with our brothers and sisters and to spend time with them as often as we are able. The more we talk about the scriptures, the stronger will be our vision, and our resolve to follow our Master.

If it is a vision we want to cultivate, then it is not enough just to read or talk about the scriptures: we also have to visualise the things we read and really make them come alive. Spending just a few minutes each day visualising not only the future, but really sensing God at work in our lives and strengthening our conviction that He is ever present, is endlessly beneficial. We might choose a Bible passage and spend time thinking about how it applies to us and what it means for the future, or we might just close our eyes and imagine what it will be like to be called away to meet our Master, to hear the words, "Well done, thou good and faithful servant ... Enter thou into the joy of thy Lord" (Matthew 25:21, KJV), and to stand with thousands upon thousands of men and women, clothed in white garments, singing praises to God and to the Lamb.

Live for the future

The stronger our conviction that God is working with us right here, right now, and is preparing something wonderful for the future, the easier it will be to live the kind of life to which we have been called. Knowing that our citizenship is in heaven (Philippians 3:20) and that we have been qualified to share in the inheritance of the saints in light (Colossians 1:12), the pleasures of this life suddenly seem so unimportant and temporary. To pursue a hedonistic lifestyle, living for ourselves rather than for God, might once have appealed; but now, knowing what the future holds, we have a far better perspective on today. No longer do we view it as an end to itself, but as a stepping stone to glory and immortality in the kingdom of God.

And so we are motivated to live for God now, even though we know this will not be easy. For we have been promised that –

> "there is no one who has left house or wife or brothers or parents or children, for the sake of the kingdom of God, who will not receive many times more in this time, and in the age to come eternal life." (Luke 18:29,30)

Most of us will probably never be called to leave behind our homes or our families, but we are certainly called to a life of sacrifice –

> "to renounce ungodliness and worldly passions, and to live self-controlled, upright, and godly lives in the present age, waiting for our blessed hope, the appearing of the glory of our great God and Saviour Jesus Christ." (Titus 2:12,13)

Choosing to do the right thing is rarely easy and often painful. We battle against the carnal mind, fed by the "all things are lawful", "anything goes" mentality so prevalent in the world. But if we are armed with a vision of greater things to come, knowing what God requires of us now and fixing our eyes on our future reward, we can stand strong and choose light over darkness – God's ways over man's ways – "work[ing] heartily, as for the Lord and not for men, knowing that from the Lord ... [we] will receive the inheritance as [our] reward" (Colossians 3:23,24).

When trials inevitably come along, our vision becomes all the more important to us. It keeps us grounded, even when the earth beneath us appears to give way. It shows us that there is a purpose to our pain. It reminds us that God will never leave us or forsake us, but will always provide us with a way of escape. And it tells us that the best is yet to come.

> "So we do not lose heart. Though our outer self is wasting away, our inner self is being renewed day by day. For this light momentary affliction is preparing for us an eternal weight of glory beyond all comparison."
> (2 Corinthians 4:16,17)

Questions and suggestions

- How clear is your vision of the future?
- How does a clear vision help in times of temptation and trial?
- Do you read the Bible every day? If not, how can you make this a part of your daily routine?
- Our vision is of the invisible. How can you make this vision real and tangible?
- Do you share your vision of the future with others? Talking about it and getting excited about it makes it so much more tangible.

Chapter 23

W for Words

AMONG God's creation, humans are unique in being able to communicate using complex language. With our words, we can encourage each other and spread the word of truth, but we can also hurt others and stumble into sin. As disciples of the Lord Jesus Christ, we must learn to bridle our tongues so that we are better able to control what we say, and discern when to say it. We need to allow the word of God to dwell in our hearts so that we do not sin against Him with our lips, but rather use our words to bring Him glory and praise.

Good treasure

Jesus said that the words we say are a reflection of the state of our hearts, and that we shall be either justified or condemned by our words (Matthew 12:37), for "out of the abundance of the heart the mouth speaks" (verse 34). If our hearts harbour even a hint of jealousy, selfishness, pride, anger, bitterness or resentment, we shall find this negativity creeping into our interactions with others, and even into our prayers. And if we delight in the pleasures of this world and allow them to take hold of our hearts, we shall find that our tongues betray where our loyalties lie. If, on the other hand, our delight is in the law of the Lord and we choose to meditate on it day and night (Psalm 1:2), we shall not be able to stop our mouths from confessing God's goodness. Our hearts will overflow with words that are pleasing to God and our speech will resound with the godly wisdom we have absorbed from the pages of scripture.

It follows, then, that if we want the right words to come out of our mouths, we must make sure the right words are going in. Although we do not literally put God's word into our mouths, it is nevertheless often described as something edible. In Revelation 10:10, John was told to eat the scroll containing the word of God, and that it was sweet as honey in his mouth, but bitter to his stomach. Similarly, in Psalm 19:10 we read that the word of God is "sweeter also than honey and drippings of the honeycomb". We know, too, that "man does not live by bread alone, but ... by every word that comes from the mouth of the LORD" (Deuteronomy 8:3). Physical food is a necessity if we are to stay alive, but spiritual food is of much more lasting value.

We ought therefore to ask ourselves a few probing questions:

- Do I put as much effort and forethought into Bible reading and study as I do into preparing and eating physical meals?
- Does my mind wander to thoughts about God's word as much as it does to thoughts about supper?
- Have I spent as much time learning how to study the Bible as I have learning how to cook?
- Do I spend more time reading and meditating on God's word, or eating physical food?
- As a family, do we place more importance on doing the readings together, or eating together?

- Am I more likely to meet up with other Christadelphians for a meal, or to do Bible study?

God has blessed us with an abundance and variety of food to eat and enjoy, and we can do so with thankfulness and need not feel guilty about doing so. But we must also recognise the importance of feasting on the word of God, since His word provides us with a kind of sustenance and satisfaction which far surpasses that of even the most delicious meal. It gives us wisdom, comfort and purpose. It teaches us how to put away jealousy and pride, how to overcome anger and resentment, and how to "walk in a manner worthy of the calling to which [we] have been called, with all humility and gentleness, with patience, bearing with one another in love" (Ephesians 4:1,2). Though we may start out with storehouses of negativity and barns full of bitterness, as we store up more and more good treasure in our hearts, we shall find that our thoughts and words are transformed, and so too our lives.

Let us therefore resolve to place our need for spiritual food above our need for physical food, and not neglect to read the scriptures each day, or to meet together to study them. God's word is living and active (Hebrews 4:12), with the power to change our lives, but it will not do so if our Bibles remain in their cases all week.

An unbridled tongue

Even with the word of God firmly implanted in our hearts, we shall still have days when we struggle to keep our words under control, since "no human being can tame the tongue" (James 3:8). Until we are free of our mortal bodies and our carnal minds, there will always be a battle inside us between the word of God and the pride of life. James rebukes his readers for their double-minded attitude: "From the same mouth come blessing and cursing" (verse 10). Are we the same? Do we enjoy gossip and unsavoury jokes one moment, and talk passionately about the Truth the next? Are we prone both to grumble and to abound with thanksgiving? Are we both boastful and humble, derisive and compassionate? "My brothers, these things ought not to be so" (verse 10).

The scriptures are very clear about the way in which we ought to speak. Our speech must "always be gracious, seasoned with salt" (Colossians 4:6), whether speaking to those inside or outside the ecclesia. Our tongues may be untameable, but this is no excuse for not trying our hardest to control what we say. Consider the following verses:

"Let every person be quick to hear, slow to speak, slow to anger." (James 1:19)

It can be easy to get angry or to speak rashly, without thinking, if we are having a bad day. Perhaps we are feeling tired, irritable or unwell. Yet there is never an excuse for anger. Aware that we are having a 'bad day', we need to be particularly careful to keep our tongues and our tempers under control, for our "rash words are like sword thrusts, but the tongue of the wise brings healing" (Proverbs 12:18). The words we say in haste are immediately painful to the hearer (and often immediately regretted by the utterer) and can cause long-lasting damage to our relationships with others, but a word spoken wisely can heal rifts and soothe troubled minds.

Sometimes, we might need to walk away from a testing situation, or at least take a few deep breaths before speaking. And if we notice that the person we are talking to is having a hard time being patient or understanding, we ought not to provoke them and make the situation worse.

"Whoever restrains his words has knowledge, and he who has a cool spirit is a man of understanding." (17:27)

When communicating with others, we can learn to listen more – to be "quick to hear" (James 1:19). Doing so ensures that the words we do speak are thoughtful, meaningful and relevant. We can talk less, but say more. And we can learn that sometimes, it is best to say nothing at all (see Ecclesiastes 3:7).

> "Let there be no filthiness nor foolish talk nor crude joking, which are out of place, but instead let there be thanksgiving." (Ephesians 5:4)

Crude joking is hard to avoid, since for many people it forms the basis of their sense of humour. In the workplace, on the television and even sometimes from the mouths of brothers and sisters, we hear dirty jokes and comments loaded with innuendo. It is becoming so commonplace that we might not bat an eyelid when we hear such talk, and may not have an issue with making similar jokes ourselves, given the "right" company. Have we become desensitised to foul language and crude talk? Then we must seek to remove as much of its influence from our lives as possible, be this reconsidering the films and TV programmes we watch, or carefully choosing the friends we spend time with, "[making] no provision for the flesh" (Romans 13:14).

Paul says that our words ought instead to be full of thanksgiving. This might seem like an unusual antidote to crude joking, but if our hearts and minds are full of gratitude for all the many blessings in this life, and for the sacrifice of our Lord Jesus which brings us eternal life, then how can we talk in such a base way? Why would we want to talk or think about all that is immoral, corrupt and dishonourable, when we could be talking and thinking about all that is true, right and honourable?

> "Let no corrupting talk come out of your mouths, but only such as is good for building up, as fits the occasion, that it may give grace to those who hear." (Ephesians 4:29)

Corrupting talk is any form of communication which tears another person down, rather than builds them up. It might make them feel sad, uncomfortable, alienated or worthless. It might shake their faith or damage their relationship with God. Few of us ever intend to hurt people's feelings, but sometimes our words might unexpectedly have a negative effect on another person. If this is the case, then we ought straight away to seek to restore peace and to sort any misunderstandings.

There are times, however, when we are not so innocent, and the motive behind our words is far more questionable. A searching examination of our motive can sometimes flag up some uncomfortable truths, hidden from all but ourselves and God. Are we really speaking to encourage a friend in need, or to share our passion for the truth; or are we seeking to impress others and to make ourselves feel important? In passing on information which a brother or sister has shared with us in confidence, are we really seeking their best interests, or merely delighting in spreading gossip? Before we speak, we ought to take a step back and ask ourselves whether we are speaking out of humility or boastfulness, compassion or spite, joy or envy. And then we must learn to hold our tongue.

The antithesis of talk which corrupts is talk which builds up and edifies. We tend to be quite good at encouraging our friends, and dishing out compliments, but is this just done to make ourselves appear likeable and kind? Is it just the socially acceptable thing to do? And are we merely building up each other's confidence and egos, or are we strengthening each other's faith?

The most encouraging conversations are those which focus on the impact of both God's word and His hand in our lives. These are conversations which we can have with all of our brothers and sisters, and everyone we meet, not just our closest friends and family. In all of our interactions, we must seek to bring God into the equation, and to speak from the heart about His very real presence in our lives.

Talk about these things

Our words ought to comfort, strengthen and inspire. Whether we are talking face-to-face, on the 'phone, writing a letter, sending an e-mail or posting on Instagram, the things we say should be said in all gentleness and meekness, with great love.

In Philippians, Paul sums up the kinds of things we should be thinking – and therefore talking – about:

> "Finally, brothers, whatever is true, whatever is honourable, whatever is just, whatever is pure, whatever is lovely, whatever is commendable, if there is any excellence, if there is anything worthy of praise, think [and talk] about these things." (Philippians 4:8)

Questions and suggestions

- What treasure do you store up in your heart? How is that evident in the way you speak?
- Do you value the gift of speech? Do you always use your tongue (or your pen / keyboard) to glorify God and to edify others, or do you sometimes use them to hurt others or to get your own way?
- Do you sometimes make excuses for the harsh words you have spoken? Perhaps you blame hormones or lack of sleep. Perhaps you were having a bad day or were feeling particularly grumpy. Perhaps you even felt that the recipient was being so annoying or unreasonable that they deserved to get an earful!

- Is there ever really an excuse?
- Does crude joking form part of your conversation with certain people? Are such words edifying or helpful? Are you setting a good example? Is this the kind of company you should be keeping (Christadelphian or not)?

Chapter 24
X for X-ray

X-RAY examinations tell us a lot about the state of our bodies. They can detect broken bones, lung problems, heart problems and even some forms of cancer. Though everything may look fine from the outside, an X-ray machine will reveal what is really going on inside our bodies.

When it comes to examining our minds, we have a far more powerful tool: the word of God. Sharper than any two-edged sword, it "discern[s] the thoughts and intentions of the heart" (Hebrews 4:12). To the onlooker, we may be doing a good job of appearing godly – we may even have persuaded ourselves that we are 'doing just fine' – but the sword of the spirit reveals who we really are inside. It highlights our pride, arrogance, envy and lust, and it does so by comparing who we are with who God is. For this reason, it is important that we regularly and honestly examine our thoughts and intentions, using the word of God as our guide.

In order to determine the damage done to our physical bodies, doctors need to know what a physically healthy body looks like. Similarly, if we are to recognise our character flaws, we need to know what a spiritually healthy body looks like. Scripture tells us how to live our lives, but the word made flesh shows us how to put this into practice. Jesus' life is the benchmark against which we must measure our thoughts and actions.

An honest spiritual X-ray will highlight that, regardless of how much progress we feel we are making, we constantly miss the mark. Try as we might, we succumb to temptation, for "the spirit indeed is willing, but the flesh is weak" (Matthew 26:41).

Reconciled by his death

What a comfort it is, then, to know that God does not hold our sinful thoughts and intentions against us but has reconciled us to Himself through the blood of His Son.

> "He does not deal with us according to our sins, nor repay us according to our iniquities. For as high as the heavens are above the earth, so great is his steadfast love toward those who fear him; as far as the east is from the west, so far does he remove our transgressions from us." (Psalm 103:10-12)

God is not blind to our sin. When He searches our hearts and tests our minds, He sees the wickedness inside each one of us. Yet, for those who are in Christ, He has chosen to "reconcile to himself all things … making peace by the blood of his [Christ's] cross" (Colossians 1:20). Though we were once "alienated and hostile in mind, doing evil deeds", we are presented "holy and blameless and above reproach before [God]" (verse 22).

When God X-rays us, He chooses to see Christ in us. Though we were dead in our trespasses, God has made us "alive together with [Christ], having forgiven all our trespasses, by cancelling the record of debt that stood against us with its legal demands.

This he set aside, nailing it to the cross" (2:13,14). God will never again call our forgiven sins to mind, or hold them against us. They have been blotted out (Acts 3:19) and trodden underfoot; cast into the depths of the sea (Micah 7:19).

But there are conditions attached to this grace and forgiveness. We only remain in Christ, "if indeed [we] continue in the faith, stable and steadfast, not shifting from the hope of the gospel that [we have] heard" (Colossians 1:23).

Things that are above

When we were baptized into Christ, we "put on Christ". All our trespasses were forgiven and we were raised from death to life. We "put on the new self" that "we too might walk in newness of life". But this was just the beginning of being a disciple of Christ, for:

> "If then you have been raised with Christ, seek the things that are above ... Put to death therefore what is earthly in you: sexual immorality, impurity, passion, evil desire, and covetousness, which is idolatry ... In these you too once walked ... But now you must put them all away: anger wrath, malice, slander, and obscene talk from your mouth."
> (Colossians 3:1,5,7,8)

Baptism does not take away natural impulses. It does not automatically change the way we think. Although God may have eliminated our sins, we still have to seek to remove all unrighteousness from our lives if we are to develop the mind of Christ (see 1 Corinthians 2:16; Philippians 2:5). To have the mind of Christ is to deny the flesh – to be utterly selfless – and to put to death all that is earthly.

Before we can begin to put to death the things of the flesh, we must recognise and acknowledge them in ourselves.

1 Corinthians 11 says: "Let a person examine himself, then, and so eat of the bread and drink of the cup" (verse 28). Each week, as we remember the Lord Jesus, we consider the perfect, sinless life he lived, serving God and others. We think of his self denial, to the extent that he gave his life for his friends. We are encouraged to take up our own cross of self-sacrifice.

This kind of spiritual X-ray is an essential part of our discipleship and ought to be something we do daily, not just at the memorial meeting. We do this by arming ourselves with "the sword of the Spirit, which is the word of God" and by looking to the example of Jesus Christ, the word made flesh. This is yet another reason why daily Bible reading is so vital for the disciple of Christ.

Goals

In an earlier chapter we considered the theme of 'goals', including a list of scriptural standards for godly living, towards which we should be aiming (see accompanying list at the end of the chapter). Consider these again and ask:

- Has there been a time recently when I have failed to keep this commandment?
- To what extent did I allow selfishness and pride to get in the way? (There is as much focus on self when we feel inferior as there is when we feel superior.)
- Can I think of a time when Jesus fulfilled this commandment?
- How might I follow his example?
- What will I do this week to put to death the old man, and to put on the mind of Christ?

Regular, honest self-examination like this is sobering and affects us in a number of ways. It might make us feel hopeless. Since we shall never be perfect, this side of the kingdom, and will inevitably give in to temptation, we might question whether there is any point in even trying to overcome the flesh and deny self. Of course there is! If we love God's law, we will desire to keep it. God asks us to serve Him with "a whole heart and a willing mind, for [He] searches all hearts and understands every plan and thought" (1 Chronicles 28:9). When God examines the heart, He does not only see faults, but also intentions. He knows where our loyalties lie. He looks for those who "live according to the Spirit" and who "set their minds on the things of the Spirit" (Romans 8:5). God compares our hearts and minds to those of the Lord Jesus, who is "the exact imprint of [God's] nature" (Hebrews 1:3). He is searching for that family likeness; for His sons and daughters who honour Him by striving to be like Him.

Far from feeling hopeless or becoming complacent, this ought to compel us to raise the expectations we have of ourselves. It is not enough to give in 'because failure is inevitable' or 'because God understands how hard this is' or 'because I know God will forgive me'. "In your struggle against sin you have not yet resisted to the point of shedding your blood" (12:4), which means we are not fighting sin as fervently as we could be. We know that "all have sinned and fall short of the glory of God" (Romans 3:23). The more we take up the sword of the Spirit and X-ray our hearts and minds, the more aware of this we become. We enter each new day determined to serve God with whole hearts and willing minds, so that He might see a part of Himself in us.

Those who are forgiven much

The alternative response is one of thankfulness, love, and not a little relief. Knowing that God understands the state of our hearts, yet has chosen us to be His sons and daughters, we can drop any façade, face our weaknesses, and pray for help to endure temptation. Sins are confessed with sorrow and humility, and we are comforted to know that the Father's forgiveness knows no limits. As we truly repent, we will be truly forgiven.

The more we can learn to search our hearts and minds and acknowledge our failings, the more aware we shall be of how loving, forgiving and merciful our Heavenly Father is; and the more aware of His love we become, the more compelled we shall feel to reciprocate that love, for those who are forgiven much, love much (Luke 7:42,43,47).

And so we are to invite God into our thoughts and hearts. To hide from Him would not only be futile, but would show a lack of trust in His love. We are to acknowledge how far short we fall and ask Him to help us to change. Our daily prayer becomes:

> "Search me, O God, and know my heart! Try me and know my thoughts! And see if there be any grievous way in me, and lead me in the way everlasting!" (Psalm 139:23,24)

I will ...

- Not be ashamed of the Gospel (Romans 1:16).
- Not let sin reign in my body (Romans 6:12).
- Delight in the law of God in my innermost being (Romans 7:22).
- Not become proud (Romans 11:20).
- Live peaceably with all (Romans 12:18).
- Glorify God in my body (1 Corinthians 6:20).
- Be free from anxieties (1 Corinthians 7:32).
- Exercise self-control in all things (1 Corinthians 9:27).

- Do everything in love (1 Corinthians 16:14).
- Not lose heart when afflicted (2 Corinthians 4:16,17).
- Widen my heart (2 Corinthians 6:13).
- Cleanse myself of every defilement of body and spirit (2 Corinthians 7:1).
- Give generously and cheerfully (2 Corinthians 8:2,3; 9:7).
- Be humble, gentle, patient and loving (Ephesians 4:2).
- Forgive others (Ephesians 4:32).
- Be thankful (Ephesians 5:4).
- Count others more significant than myself (Philippians 2:3,4).
- Not grumble (Philippians 2:15).
- Rejoice in the Lord always (Philippians 4:4).
- Learn to be content in all situations (Philippians 4:11).
- Seek the things that are above (Colossians 3:1).
- Not be angry (Colossians 3:8).
- Do everything in the name of the Lord Jesus, giving thanks to God through him (Colossians 3:17).
- Work heartily, as for the Lord and not for men (Colossians 3:23).
- Make the best use of time (Colossians 4:5).
- Not speak to please man, but to please God (1 Thessalonians 2:4).
- Control my body in holiness and honour, not filled with lust (1 Thessalonians 4:4,5).
- Live quietly, minding my own business (1 Thessalonians 4:11).
- Encourage the fainthearted; help the weak (1 Thessalonians 5:14).

- Pray without ceasing (1 Thessalonians 5:17).
- Not quarrel, but be kind to everyone (2 Timothy 2:24).
- Patiently reprove, rebuke and exhort (2 Timothy 4:2).
- Be submissive to rulers and authorities (Titus 3:1).
- Speak evil of no one (Titus 3:2).
- Keep my life free from love of money and be content with what I have (Hebrews 13:5).

Recommended reading: Dennis Gillett – *The Genius of Discipleship*, Chapter 1: "Be Ye Transformed".

Questions and suggestions

- Do you examine your motives, thoughts and behaviour on a daily and weekly basis? Is your examination thorough or regular enough?
- What areas in your life require improvement?
- Do you feel ashamed and repentant when your conscience is pricked, or do you put up defensive barriers?
- Perhaps you no longer feel bad about a particular sin. How could the sword of the Spirit – the word of God – help here?
- How hard do you really try to avoid giving in to temptation? It is unlikely that you have "yet resisted to the point of shedding your blood" (Hebrews 12:4).
- What one step forward will you take this week?

Chapter 25 — Y for Yoke

WHEN Jesus said, "Take my yoke upon you and learn from me ..." (Matthew 11:29), this was a call to action. He did not promise to take away our yoke, but has rather freed us from the heavy yoke of captivity to sin and invites us to share his yoke.

The yoke of Christ

But what does it mean to be yoked to Christ? He has told us that his yoke is easy and his burden is light (verse 30), but how do we apply this knowledge to our own lives? Although the terms "yoke" and "burden" are sometimes used interchangeably – meaning something we have to bear – we learn two separate lessons from this verse in Matthew. Firstly, a yoke binds two animals together, so that they can carry a load together. As followers and imitators of the Lord Jesus Christ, we are yoked to him and we share the load.

Our English Bibles, perhaps confusingly, describe this yoke as being "easy". *Thayer's Greek Lexicon* tells us that this can mean 'useful' and 'manageable', but also 'pleasant' or 'mild' (as opposed to 'harsh', 'sharp' or 'bitter'). It is an interesting exercise to look at how the same Greek word has been translated elsewhere. We find it in the following verses:

- "... God's *kindness* [KJV, *goodness*] is meant to lead you to repentance" (Romans 2:4).
- "Be *kind* to one another ..." (Ephesians 4:32).
- "... if indeed you have tasted that the Lord is *good* [KJV, *gracious*]" (1 Peter 2:3).

If we place these words in the context of Matthew 11, we see that the yoke we share with Christ is one of kindness and goodness, and it makes our burdens easier to bear. Though the world might tell us that faith in God is futile, stifling and merely holds us back, we know that being yoked to Christ actually helps us to move forward, taking significant weight off our shoulders.

To be yoked to the world is to be bound to the very thing that holds us back and causes us to stumble, and with this yoke we must carry such heavy burdens. Like the scribes and the Pharisees, the world "[ties] up heavy burdens, hard to bear, and [lays] them on people's shoulders" (Matthew 23:4), but "the LORD has laid on [Christ] the iniquity of us all" (Isaiah 53:6). This heavy burden of sin and death has been taken away from all who have chosen to bind themselves to Christ and to take up his yoke.

Nevertheless, we have not been promised an easy journey; there is still a burden to bear. Yet Jesus says that his burden is light (Matthew 11:30), and this same word is used by the Apostle Paul in 2 Corinthians 4, where we read:

> "For this slight [light, KJV] momentary affliction is preparing for us an eternal weight of glory beyond all comparison." (verse 17)

Here is our assurance and with Christ by our side, sharing the load, we know we shall always have the strength to bear it.

Out of Egypt

As slaves to the Egyptians, the Israelites carried out back-breaking work day after day. Just when they thought things couldn't get any worse, they were told that they would no longer be given straw to make bricks, but would have to gather it themselves, though they would still be expected to meet their daily quota and would be beaten if they failed (Exodus 5:10-14). These were impossible working conditions and the people staggered under the weight of this heavy burden.

It seems almost unthinkable, then, that the Israelites should so soon forget how hard their lives as slaves had been. The Lord God had brought them out of Egypt – freeing them from the yoke of Pharaoh – with a mighty hand and an outstretched arm (Deuteronomy 4:34). Pharaoh and his army were now at the bottom of the sea, broken and utterly powerless. Yet freedom, they soon realised, was not as wonderful as they had imagined it would be. Surrounded by harsh, desert conditions, constantly moving from one place to the next, they could not build beautiful homes and settle down to a life of luxury. Then there was the constant threat of attack, for they were wandering through arid wilderness, carrying valuable stores of water, along with their livestock and a great deal of gold and jewellery.

And there were so many rules! They soon found out that they couldn't worship God in the way the Egyptians had worshipped their gods. They couldn't just do as they pleased, but were given strict commandments concerning every aspect of daily life. Not only that, but there were severe punishments for disobedience. What a chore it all was. They didn't feel free at all!

So when the twelve spies returned from spying out the land of Canaan, weighed down with grapes, pomegranates and figs, and full of stories of a land flowing with milk and honey (Numbers 13:23,27), we can well understand why the people began to murmur. They lacked the faith to believe that God would bring them safely into this new and fruitful land, but at the same time they were reminded of the lush, green vegetation of the Fertile Crescent, and the abundant variety of fruit and vegetables which they had enjoyed there. True, they had been slaves, whose cruel taskmasters had worked them hard, but at least they were relatively safe, and they had food and drink. They had enjoyed many aspects of Egyptian culture and worship. Was it really so bad? Besides, they had been victorious over Pharaoh and his army. Suddenly, the idea didn't seem so far-fetched. Perhaps they could return to Egypt and make a fresh start, living side by side with the people there, as they had in the days of Joseph.

Slaves of obedience

Are we so different? When the Israelites crossed the Red Sea, they were redeemed from the hand of the Egyptians and given new life. The captors were swallowed up by the very same act that set the captives free. In the same way, when Jesus died, death was swallowed up in victory and, at the same time, many captives were set free. God has brought us out of spiritual Egypt, setting us free from the law of sin and death (Romans 8:2). We were "dead in the trespasses and sins in which [we] once walked, following the course of this world ... carrying out the desires of the body and the mind ... like the rest of mankind" (Ephesians 2:1-3), but through Christ we have been "brought from death to life" (Romans 6:13) and have been made "alive together with Christ" (Ephesians 2:5). We can see the Promised Land in our mind's eye. Do we truly want to be there, or do we – like the Israelites – feel pulled towards the pleasures of this life, from which we have been set free?

Why then do we continue to indulge the flesh? Our natural response to freedom is to run straight back into captivity; to return to spiritual Egypt and to "submit again to a yoke of slavery" (Galatians 5:1). Our spiritual response to freedom is to yoke ourselves to Christ, working together with him to glorify God as "slaves of ... obedience, which leads to righteousness" (Romans 6:16). Being set free in order to be a slave might seem contradictory, but we know that there is no lasting happiness or peace to be found in serving sin – in serving self. When we were slaves of sin, we were free to do as we pleased, but "the end of those things is death" and we were not bearing fruit (verses 20,21). Now that we have chosen to put on Christ and to submit to his yoke, becoming slaves of God, we know that the fruit we bear leads to sanctification and eternal life (verse 22).

Walk by the Spirit

We are exhorted in Galatians not to use our freedom as an opportunity to serve the flesh, but as an opportunity to serve one another through love (5:13). Rules, laws and traditions "are of no value in stopping the indulgence of the flesh" (Colossians 2:23), but if we "walk by the Spirit, [we] will not gratify the desires of the flesh" (Galatians 5:16). For "to set the mind on the flesh is death, but to set the mind on the Spirit is life and peace" (Romans 8:6).

Perhaps, as it did to the Israelites, this all seems impossibly hard to us. To walk by the Spirit and not gratify the desires of the flesh is to deny ourselves so many things. Perhaps we look around us and sometimes envy those who do not know God, and the carefree way in which they indulge their every whim without a second thought. They can say what they like, do as they please, and fulfil their every lust and pleasure. Rather than feeling guilty about their hedonism, they revel in it and encourage others to do the same. It makes them feel alive, but they do not realise that, spiritually, they are dead: without hope, unless they turn to God.

Whenever we begin to envy the way of life which the world presents in such an appealing way – whenever we are tempted to gratify the desires of the flesh – we must remember that God knows what is best for His children. He knows that we need structure and discipline in order to make the most of life. Partying, self-promotion, building bigger barns, selfish relationships – none of these things will bring us lasting contentment. We know from the ever-increasing rates of stress, anxiety, depression and suicide that the world does not have the answers, no matter how good its marketing team might be. The world's yoke is heavy and its grip is tight. The narrow path is not easy to tread, but it is far better to walk the narrow path, yoked to Christ, than to drag the weight of the world along the broad way that leads to destruction.

What a privilege it is, then, to be yoked to Christ as we journey through life. Not only does he share the load, but he also guides us along the right path. "Learn from me", he implored (Matthew 11:29). As a true slave of righteousness, he has set us the ultimate example of obedience to God. Though tempted, like us, to enjoy the pleasures of sin, he refused to yoke himself to the world. Instead, he set his mind on spiritual things. We, too, must regularly and earnestly feed our spiritual mind with the word of God and starve our fleshly mind of opportunities for feasting. We are to keep in step with the Spirit (Galatians 5:16), imitating Christ's "faith working through love" (verse 6).

So whose slave are you? Are you in step with the Spirit, or with the flesh? Have you truly turned your back on spiritual Egypt, or is there a part of you that longs to go back? Do you indulge the flesh, or deny it? Are you yoked to Christ, or to the world? We show by our works whose we are. "If we live by the Spirit, let us also walk by the Spirit" (verse 25).

Questions and suggestions

- What is the yoke of Christ? Are you yoked to him or to the world?
- Through Christ, you have been set free from the chains of sin and death – but do you really want that freedom, or does sin still have a hold on your heart?
- Whose slave are you, and whose do you want to be?
- What kind of fruit are you bearing?
- What steps can you take in order to stop gratifying the desires of the flesh? What can you put into your life and what must you push out or let go of?

Chapter 26: Z for Zeal

OVER the course of these chapters, we have considered many different aspects of discipleship and have hopefully been encouraged to implement some positive changes in our lives. But are we doing so enthusiastically, or only half-heartedly? Are we feeling motivated, or do we lack the drive to see things through? Are we zealous for good works (Titus 2:14)? Are we zealous for God (Acts 22:3)?

Finding your cause

The dictionary definition of zeal is "great energy or enthusiasm in pursuit of a cause or an objective". We feel the greatest energy and enthusiasm for the things we most believe in; the causes that most resonate with us. So the first question to ask ourselves is: what is my greatest cause or objective in life? What am I really passionate about?

- Preaching the word?
- Studying God's word?

- Helping those in need?
- Developing a godly character?
- Manifesting God's purpose and values to the world?
- Teaching my children the way of the Lord?
- Supporting my ecclesia?
- Or something else entirely?

Energy and enthusiasm are exhaustible resources, so we need to channel them in the right direction. If our greatest objective in life is to earn more money, to grow a successful business, to travel the world, or any number of other things which do not hold eternal weight, now is the time to consider carefully our priorities. We cannot be zealous for the things of this life, and for the things of God.

However, knowing your cause and pursuing it are two different things. We can have grand ideas and high ideals, but unless we turn these into actions, they are meaningless. Many times in scripture we read the phrase, "the zeal of the LORD of hosts will do [KJV, perform] this" (e.g., 2 Kings 19:31; Isaiah 9:7). Zeal is an active characteristic. It gets things done.

Creating an action plan

If zeal is made manifest in our actions, then it follows that we need to have an action plan. Consider the following questions in the context of ecclesial life, and your own discipleship:

- What are my core values and beliefs?
- What really motivates and excites me?
- Where do my strengths lie?
- How could I really make a difference?
- What, therefore, could be my main cause or objective right now?

- What are my first steps? (What do I need to do, and what do I need to stop doing?)
- What obstacles should I be prepared to face, and how will I overcome them?
- How will I know if I've been successful? (Do I have a clear vision or goal?)

Our answers to these questions will be as diverse as we are, and our determination and zeal will manifest itself in many different ways. Some of us will get actively involved in preaching; others into organising fellowship events. Some will open their homes to their brothers and sisters, showing great hospitality and kindness; still others will find joy in teaching Sunday School or in encouraging young people in their Bible study. Some will share their enthusiasm for God's word from the platform; others will do so in conversation over a cup of tea. Yet, because the source of our values and objectives is the same – the word of God – we shall work as one, united in purpose and strength, doing all to the glory of God (1 Corinthians 10:31).

In the ideal ecclesia, every brother or sister will know how to play to their strengths, whilst being open to trying new things and to taking on new roles and responsibilities where there is a need. Each member will have clear sight of their shared values and spiritual objectives, and will encourage others to "work heartily, as for the Lord" (Colossians 3:23).

Because they believe in their cause, can relate to it, and feel equipped to pursue it, every member of the ecclesia will undertake it with passion, energy, enthusiasm and zeal. In such an ecclesia, no individual brother or sister will bear the burden of encouraging and enthusing the whole ecclesia. No one will feel duty-bound to muster the zeal of ten men in order to make up for a lack of enthusiasm from other members. No one will feel under constant pressure to do everything and resolutely to fit every mould. Everyone will have a purpose and will pursue it with zeal.

Fostering the right environment

Realistically, however, we know that no one is able to remain enthusiastic and full of zeal all of the time. A certain degree of apathy affects even the most enthusiastic of disciples from time to time – especially when they feel particularly overworked or underworked. So how can we make sure that our ecclesial environment is one which encourages everyone to increase in zeal for good works and for the word of God? Here are just a few of the obstacles we might face, along with some suggestions for positive change:

The same few people do all the work and others either feel their help is not needed, or are happy to take a back seat.

- The arranging brethren could ask each ecclesial member where they feel their strengths lie, and what they would like to do to get involved – then create opportunities for them.
- All members are encouraged to attend committee meetings so that they feel included, represented, and can share their ideas and expertise.
- Those who are frequently busy within the ecclesia could delegate to those who do less, and not be afraid to ask for practical help from those who do not actively get involved. (Perhaps they feel excluded or that their help is not needed, or just need some encouragement.)

Cliques have formed; some people feel excluded and are therefore less willing to get involved.

- Create opportunities for fellowship – always including a spiritual element – on both a larger and a smaller scale (fellowship days versus inviting someone round for coffee).

- If you have a task to do (teaching in Sunday School, billing for a special preaching effort, visiting someone in hospital, catering for a fraternal, speaking at a Bible School at home or abroad), ask someone you wouldn't normally ask to help or accompany you.

Vision has dimmed; enthusiasm for God's word has waned.

- Organise a series of weekly or monthly study classes, led by an enthusiastic and knowledgeable speaker, with a communal meal afterwards where discussion is encouraged.
- Start a home study class, book club or reading group, and be inclusive about whom you invite. (Larger ecclesias could divide into smaller groups for study classes, making sure there is a good mix of backgrounds and ages.)

We all have a responsibility to keep our own flames burning, and to help fan each other's flames when they are in danger of going out. How we do this is determined on a case-by-case basis, but the most important thing is that we keep on doing it!

We must never assume that a brother or sister who appears to have lost all enthusiasm is a lost cause. After all, if you were in their position, you would surely hope that your brothers and sisters would work together to pull you out of the rut and help you to rediscover your passion for the things of God.

By finding ways to involve everyone in the ecclesia, and by initiating open, honest, friendly, spiritually-driven (but unintimidating) conversations, we can begin to foster a positive environment in which vision and zeal can grow.

Zeal is infectious. The more we work on strengthening our vision and enthusiasm for God's word, the greater will be our ability to spread this enthusiasm.

Loving good, hating evil

Being zealous is not just about showing zeal for what is good, but about zealously hating evil and turning from it. "Love must be sincere. Hate what is evil; cling to what is good" (Romans 12:9, NIV). If our love for God is genuine, we shall hate what He hates and love what He loves.

But is this truly the case for you and for me? Do we hate evil so much that we are prepared to go to extreme lengths to rid it from our midst, or do we tolerate a certain amount of worldly influence within the ecclesia and within our own lives? Humanism and self-worship have become so normalised, but God hates these things. He hates it when we put our own needs before those of others, and allow pride and ego to take over; when we continually rank Him second or third in our lives after ourselves, our friends, our work or our precious free time; when tolerance and a desire to move with the times become more important than obedience to His unchanging word; and when we lower our standards or adjust our values to accommodate the world's ever-changing views.

Have we become desensitised to the things God hates? Has the concept of hatred become so taboo, in a society which tolerates almost anything, that we are unwilling to hate what God hates? Are we prepared to take up God's cause and zealously hate what He hates and love what He loves?

Our first-century brothers and sisters faced this same challenge. The brothers and sisters in Thyatira were zealous for good works (Revelation 2:19), but were criticised by the Lord Jesus for their lack of zeal when it came to casting out the influences of sexual immorality and idolatry (verse 20). On the other hand, though commended for their zealous hatred of evil (verse 2), those in Ephesus had abandoned their first love (verse 4) and ceased doing good works (verse 5). Meanwhile, those in Sardis enjoyed a great reputation from outsiders for good works – yet spiritually, they were dead (3:1). And the lukewarm Laodiceans? Driven more by an appetite for financial gain (verse 17) than by a humble, genuine zeal for the things of God, their faith went only skin deep.

The stark warnings given to these ecclesias are as relevant to us today as they were then:

- No amount of good works will make up for a heart that is full of idolatry and immorality.
- It is therefore not enough zealously to love good; we must also zealously hate evil and seek to rid it from our lives.
- Yet hating what God hates profits little if this does not stir us up to do good works.
- God is not fooled by false piety and an outward show of good works; true zeal comes from within.
- Reputation, money and hatred are not to be our motivation for good works; rather, a genuine desire to do good, to love others and to glorify God.
- God asks for all or nothing – zeal or no zeal!

Fleeing from idolatry

Of course, it would be hypocritical of us to storm zealously into our respective ecclesial halls and demand that others renounce all ungodliness and idolatry. We know very little of what goes on inside the minds and hearts of our brothers and sisters, yet know only too well our own struggle with sin. The hard work begins with you and with me:

> "You hypocrite, first take the log out of your own eye, and then you will see clearly to take the speck out of your brother's eye." (Matthew 7:5)

We know that our God is a jealous God, zealous for His people (1 Kings 19:10; Psalm 78:58). He will not tolerate the idols we store up in our hearts, and neither should we. He asks for our whole hearts and minds – for all of our energy, enthusiasm and zeal. Nothing should come between us and God – not least our own pride and selfishness. Whether it is a lifestyle choice, an addiction, a character trait, a career choice or a hobby that seeks to draw us away from God, we must aggressively rid our lives of these things. We live in a tolerant society, but we must not apply this tolerance to our own sin – or indeed the sins of our brothers and sisters.

When Jehu destroyed the house of Ahab and all the Baal worshippers, he didn't do so apologetically or timidly. "Come with me, and see my zeal for the LORD", was his faithful declaration (2 Kings 10:16). When Jesus made a whip of cords and drove the money-changers from the temple (John 2:15), he didn't go about it quietly and calmly. Zeal for God's house had consumed him (verse 17; Psalm 69:9). When God saw that there was no justice and that there was no one to intercede for His people (Isaiah 59:15,16), He did not stand by and do nothing: "He put on garments of vengeance for clothing, and wrapped himself in zeal as a cloak" (verse 17).

How great is your zeal for the Lord? What is consuming you? The desires of the flesh, or a desire to obey God? Are you ready to wrap yourself in a cloak of godly zeal and give yourself over wholly to the Lord your God?

Whether we are pursuing the things God loves, or ridding our lives of the things He hates, may we never be "slothful in zeal" but rather be "fervent in spirit" (Romans 12:11). Let us "consider how to stir up one another to love and good works ... and all the more as [we] see the Day drawing near" (Hebrews 10:24,25).

Questions and suggestions

- What are you really passionate about? In which area of your life do you show the most zeal?
- What are your core values? What really drives you?
- How could you use this passion, drive and zeal to benefit God and the ecclesia?
- What obstacles are you facing and how might they be overcome?
- Do you love what God loves and hate what He hates? Is this evident in the way you live your life?
- Is there anything in your life that is drawing you away from God? Are you prepared to get rid of it?
- Are you ready to give God your all?

Scripture index

Genesis
1:3 11
 :27 21
6:5 84
12:2,7 77
15:6 77
17:1,2 78
 :9-14 78
 :21 78
20:6 54

Exodus
4:12 148
 :13 148
5:2 72
 :10-14 177
16:12 70
19:5 134
21 .... 82, 83
 :1-6 81
 :5 82
 :6 82
31:13 70
33:17 69
34:6,7 71

Numbers
13:23,27 178
 :30 96
14:6-8 96

Deuteronomy
4:34 177
 :35 70
6:4 69
7:6-8 76
 :9 124
8:2 103
 :3 160
 :11-14,17 28
12:7,18 61
13:4,6-10 79
17:1 132
26:11 61
30:6 79
33:26,27 109

Joshua
1:8 89
4:14 30

1 Samuel
1:8 .... 127, 129
 :15 129
 :17 129
2:1 29
15:3 73
 :22 133

2 Samuel
22:49 30

1 Kings
8:23,24 124
9:4 54
14:7 30
19:10 189

2 Kings
10:16 189
19:31 183

1 Chronicles
28:9 171
29:11 27
 :14 27

2 Chronicles

29 :3 96
32 :23 30

Nehemiah

3 :28 58
4 :7,8 57
:9 57
:13 57
:14,20 57
:16 58
8 :10 62
12 :27 141
:31 141

Job

1 :21 30
2 :3 .... 54, 56
:9 56
3 :4 12
:20 12
36 :26 74
37 :14 116

Psalms

1 22
:2 160
9 :1 139
18 65
:29 130
19 :10 .... 86, 160
:14 84
20 :7,8 127
21 :13 25
22 65
23 :1-3 118
24 :1 70
26 :1 59

27 :1 88
:4 10
28 :7 141
31 65
37 :7 118
:23,24 43
:24 105
:25,26 104
40 :8 136
41 65
42 :1 65
:11 128
48 :2 67
:9 89
49 :3 86
50 :5 133
:23 133
51 :17 133
55 :22 20
56 :13 12
57 :5 26
62 :2 56
69 :9 189
77 :2 128
:12 89
78 :58 189
84 :11 3
86 :12 143
89 15-17 29
:19 30
91 :15,16 124
102 :4 128
:27,28 128
103 :10-12 168
:12 .... 44, 52
113 :4 26
116 :17 133
119 :11 .... 19, 90

:15,99 89
:27 89
:105 .... 12, 13
:148 89
:162 66
121 :4 6
136 :1 138
138 :2 26
139 :2,3 69
:7,8 7
:11,12 14
:23,24 .... 15, 172
141 :2 133
145 :5 89
:14 127
148 :13 26
149 :2 67

Proverbs

3 :5 .... 2, 126
:5,6 21
:28 94
12 :18 162
13 :4 93
14 :23 94
17 :27 162
20 :1 18
:4 93
21 :3 133
24 :30-34 93
29 :18 152

Ecclesiastes

1 :9 64
2 :17 30
3 :7 163
:9,12,13 120
:22 62
4 :6 119

Scripture index | 193

5:1 133
:12 120
:19 63
9:10 93
11:4 96

Song of Solomon

4:7 52

Isaiah

2:2,3 67
:3 75
:11 31
9:7 183
12:4 31
35:1,2 67
:10 67
43:4 52
:10 70
:13 70
45:5 69
52:13 30
53:6 176
55:9 112
59:15,16 189
:17 189
61:10 66
62:5 66
65:17-19 67
66:2 108

Jeremiah

1:6 148
2:2 81
:32 81
4:4 79
17:9 48
23:24 6

24:6,7 74
29:13 107
31:3 81
:33,34 75

Lamentations

3:25-28 118

Ezekiel

12:25 125
16:59 81
:60,62 82
24:14 125

Daniel

4:17 30

Hosea

6:6 133
13:4 69
:6 28

Micah

7:19 .... 44, 169

Habakkuk

2:14 75

Zechariah

2:10 67

Matthew

5:14 .... 11, 72
:22 49
:28 49
:40,41 49
:48 49
6:2 30

:25-32 3
:33 23
7:5 188
:13 104
11 176
:29 .... 175, 180
:30 .... 175, 176
12:34 159
:37 159
14:23 116
16:24 136
19:26 70
21:22 20
23:4 176
:12 29
:27,28 48
25:21 .... 67, 156
:40 147
26:41 .... 19, 168

Mark

7:21,22 85
9:41 8
10:30 30
12:30 23

Luke

3:14 63
6:45 85
7:42,43,47 172
10:20 66
:27 104
12:7 52
15:6,7 66
18:9 47
:9-14 47
:14 48
:29,30 157
21:28 106

John

1:29 66
2:15 189
:17 189
3:16,17 135
8:12 11
10:9 83
12:46,36 13
14:6 13
15:11 64
17:3 .... 70, 75

Acts

1:24 69
3:19 169
22:3 182

Romans

1:16 .... 44, 172
2:4 176
:15 43
3:23 171
:27,28 43
5:2 66
:3-5 .... 4, 102, 105, 140
6:11 44
:12 .... 44, 172
:13 178
:16 179
:16-22 82
:20,21 179
:22 179
:23 72
7:18 43
:22 .... 43, 44, 172
8:2 .... 50, 178
:5 171
:6 179

:18 4
:28 102
:30 77
:32 52
:39 52
11:20 .... 44, 172
12:1 135
:2 .... 85, 136
:9 187
:11 189
:18 .... 44, 172
13:12 13
:14 163

1 Corinthians

1:26,27,29,31 149
2:9 154
:16 .... 8, 169
4:1,5 14
6:13 18
:19 21
:20 .... 44, 172
7:32 .... 44, 172
8:13 34
9:25 45
:27 172
10:13 105
:31 .... 7, 184
11:28 170
12:7 150
:20 150
13 76
:12 74
15:28 154
16:13 45
:14 173

2 Corinthians

1:10 103
4:4 13

:6 72
:16,17 .... 45, 158, 173
:17 176
5:7 153
:14,15 7
:20 7
6:13 .... 45, 173
7:1 .... 45, 173
8:2,3 .... 45, 173
9:7 .... 45, 173
12:9 108
:10 .... 63, 149

Galatians

2:20 7
3:27 41
5:1 179
:6 180
:13 179
:16 .... 179, 180
:19-21 15
:19,21 18
:22,23 .... 15, 41
:25 180
6:9 9

Ephesians

1:4,5 77
:16 142
2:1-3 178
:5 178
4:1,2 161
:1-3 8
:2 .... 45, 173
:23,24 90
:29 163
:32 .... 45, 173, 176
5:2 133
:4 .... 45, 163, 173
:8 12

Scripture index | 195

:11-14 15
:15,16 92
:20 139
6:5 63
:13-17 58

Philippians

2:3 .... 34, 99, 109, 146
:3,4 .... 45, 173
:5 .... 146, 169
:14,15 45
:15 173
:16 13
3:1 45
:8 134
:9-11 40
:13 10
:13,14 .... 43, 155
:20 157
4:4 .... 45, 173
:7 4
:8 .... 91, 165
:9 91
:11 .... 45, 63, 173
:11,12 100
:18 133
:19 104

Colossians

1:12 .... 143, 157
:20 168
:22 168
:23 169
2:13,14 169
:23 179
3:1 .... 45, 173
:1,2 155
:1,5,7,8 169
:2 44
:3 .... 9, 21
:5 173
:8 45

:15 9
:16 66
:17 .... 8, 45
:23 .... 7, 45, 120, 173, 184
:23,24 157
4:5 .... 45, 173
:6 162

1 Thessalonians

2:4 .... 45, 173
4:4,5 .... 45, 173
:11 .... 45, 120, 173
:16 83
5:5 11
:14 .... 45, 173
:16 62
:17 .... 46, 174
:18 141
:21 73
:24 124

2 Thessalonians

1:3 142
3:11,12 120

1 Timothy

5:1,2 34
6:17 62

2 Timothy

1:9 52
2:24 .... 46, 174
4:2 .... 46, 174
:8 44

Titus

1:2 153
:16 71
2:12,13 157

:14 182
3:1 .... 46, 174
:2 .... 46, 174

Hebrews

1:3 171
4:12 ..... 112, 161, 167
9:28 66
10:24,25 189
11 55
:1 153
:6 72
:10 153
:25 153
:26 153
:27 153
12:1,2 44
:2 65
:4 171
:5 2
:6,7 101
:10 .... 2, 140
:11 2
13:5 .... 46, 174
:15 133

James

1:2 140
:3,4 3
:4 57
:12 3
:19 .... 162, 163
2:17 41
3:8 161
:10 162
4:8 112
5:16 112

1 Peter

1:6 57

2:2 86
:3 176
:9 .... 12, 21
4:12,13 64
:13 65
5:7 105
:9 105
:10 105

1 John

3:1 71
:2 21
4:8 71

2 John

1:12 103

3 John

1:13,14 103

Revelation

2:2 187
:4 187
:5 187
:7 154
:10 44
:11 154
:17 154
:19 187
:20 187
:26-28 154
3:1 188
:5 154
:12 154
:17 188
:20 83
:21 154
7:14 52
10:10 160
21:4 106
:23 11
22:5 11